ALSO BY RICHARD DEGRANDPRE

Ritalin Nation: Rapid-Fire Culture and the Transformation

of Human Consciousness

Digitopia

RICHARD DeGRANDPRE

DIGITOPIA

The Look of the New Digital You

NEW YORK

Library of Congress Cataloging-in-Publication Data

DeGrandpre, Richard J.
Digitopia : the look of the new digital you / Richard DeGrandpre.
p.   cm.
ISBN 0-8129-9156-7
1. Computers and civilization.   I. Title.

QA76.9.C66 D44 2001
303.48'34—dc21   00-068327

Printed in the United States of America on acid-free paper

Website address: www.atrandom.com

2 4 6 8 9 7 5 3

First Edition

Like the nomadic hordes wandering across an ancient desert in search of the soul's oasis, graphic man embraces the pleasures of barbarism and swears fealty to the sovereignty of the moment.

Lewis Lapham

Welcome to the desert of the real.

Jean Baudrillard

Preface

Is Bill Gates your man of the future? I sure hope not. Like many proponents of the digital age, he sees an electronic utopia ahead and pays little or no attention to the social and ecological world being left behind. Gates and his ilk point us in the direction of a new digital dreamworld. But as I attempt to show in this book, this vision is really a mirage, and one that traps us within a seductive but ultimately false sense of empowerment. In his book *The Road Ahead,* Gates writes, "I used to date a woman who lived in a different city. We spent a lot of time together on e-mail. And we figured out a way we could sort of go to the movies together. We would find a film that was playing about the same time in both our cities. We would drive to our respective theaters, chatting on our cellular phones. We would watch the movies and on the way home we would use our cellular phones again to discuss the show. In the future this sort of virtual dating will be better because the movie watching will be combined with video conference." Is this the virtual reality you plan for your future?

As an antidote to our ever more thoughtless and vigorous pursuit of a fully wired (and wireless) world, I offer here a panoramic guide to the psychology of the digital age—an exploration into the dark side of the emerging digital culture and the life of the mind it's now creating. The overall story is spread over twenty-five essays organized into five uneven parts.

The first of these parts throws the reader into the thick of it, exploring the nature of digitization and showing why the digital future will be unlike anything that has come before. This is because digitization spawns new technologies that allow us to break both nature and reality into interchangeable parts, and then reconstitute those parts into whole new creations. The result will be a world fabricated of simulated reality and synthetic nature.

The book's second part locates our digital future in a larger context by looking at the historical origins underlying its logic and momentum. This involves a consideration of the ways in which media technologies have transformed human consciousness in the past, beginning with the appearance of spoken language—the most powerful information technology of all time.

With these first two parts acting as a foundation, Part III gets to the heart of the matter by providing a close-up look at ten different facets of the new digital you. These facets, or themes, were chosen because each is clearly expressed in contemporary American society and because each will become an even more defining aspect of American life as we move further into the digital information age. It is here that I attempt to tear away the hypnotic lens through which you look to the digital future, replacing it with what I hope will be a clearer account of what it will mean, and what it already means, for you to inhabit a world gone digital.

Finally, Parts IV and V turn our attention to the prospect of building and inhabiting the digital dreamworld I have called *digitopia*. What is digitopia? It is at this time only an imaginary place, a place located somewhere off in the digital future. It is constituted in our collective dreams for a fully wired (and wireless) world, and it is founded upon an ethos that imbues all that is electronic with vitality, influence, and importance. Simply, digitopia is a metaphor for the utopian otherworld that we are setting our sights on as we abandon hope for the present world. Part IV evaluates the geography of this digitopia, a simulated and thus infinite realm spread out across a placeless space and a timeless time. Lastly, in the fifth and final section of the book I look at certain social structures that both promote and reinforce the look of the new digital you.

—

Comments, both hot and cold, may be sent to:
digitopia2001@hotmail.com.

—

Richard DeGrandpre
Burlington, Vermont
October 15, 2000

Contents

Preface   ix

PART I. GOING DIGITAL

Introduction   3
some coming attractions
Digitally Mastered   8
on the nature and meaning of all that is digital
Four DNA Bases, Twenty-six Letters, a Zero, and a One   14
how code continues to take over the world
The One and Only Reality   19
not appreciating what reality really is, we have squandered
its substance and materiality
The Real and the True   26
how the academics' debate over objectivity and truth missed
the point
Surviving *Survivor*   31
how to survive when lost between virtual reality and real
virtuality
Digital Mechanics   36
measuring the impact of the digital revolution

PART II. THE LONG JOURNEY INTO DIGITOPIA

A Short History of the Digital Self   43
  *first stripped naked, then jacked in, and soon to be
  downloaded*
Unplugged Media   49
  indigenous oral cultures and the first four selves
Plugged-in Media   57
  child of projection: the fifth self
The Coming of Digital Age   63
  cyberpunks and the sixth self

PART III. THE PSYCHOLOGY OF THE DIGITAL AGE

A Digital Ethos   69
  just log on, jack in, and drop out
The Sad and Lonely World of Cyberspace   75
  *what psychological research can (and cannot) tell us about
  america online*
Virtual Reality Shapes the Mind in Its Own Image   82
  a psychological theory of why virtuality rules
A Digital Virus   87
  how the digital revolution feeds off a crippled social sphere
Fight and Flight   94
  *instead of fighting for a better world, we're taking flight into
  virtuality*

The Drama of the Digital Self   100

no more struggle between the will to power and the need
for mutual recognition

Digital Dreams, Concrete Realities   105

how the desires of the plugged-in world spill over into
everyday life

Feeling Oh, So Analog in an All-Too-Digital Age   111

why faster computers and better graphics will never be
enough

The Incredible Shrinking Attention Span   117

how you accommodate yourself to a distracted way of life

Pharmacological Aid   123

on our way to digitopia, drugs have become prosthetics for a
self under siege

PART IV. THE GEOGRAPHY OF DIGITOPIA

Living in Timeless Time and Placeless Space   133

in search of place in the age of cyberspace

Constructing Digitopia   140

making our digital dreamworld a technological reality

PART V. THE FUTURE OF THE FUTURE

The (Bill) Joys of Technology   155

fearing the future that already is

Our Fantastic Voyage   164

> *wild ride or technological tailspin: can we tell the difference?*

Acknowledgments   171

Notes   173

PART I

GOING DIGITAL

To high speed change no adjustment is possible. We become spectators only and must escape into understanding.

Marshall McLuhan[1]

INTRODUCTION

some coming attractions

Marshall McLuhan redefined the nature and influence of media when he declared in 1964 that *the medium is the message.* It's not *what* you're watching that's important, McLuhan told us, it's *that* you're watching. As visionary as McLuhan was of the electronic age, he could hardly have anticipated the meaning his message would have for us only four decades later, basking as we are today in the dawn of a digital age. Cyberspace and its World Wide Web, cell phones and other modes of wireless communication, new digital devices for music, video, video games, and television—these are the portals through which we are entering a new digital age. As these new modes of experience suggest, going digital represents a revolutionary breakthrough in our capacity to extend, simulate, and re-create what was once the one and only reality. In doing so it opens up the possibility of our hypergliding down a path we have long been traveling, one that ends with both mind and matter downloaded into a virtual machine. Left unchecked, the ultimate irony of our unbridled attempt to master all of nature, save our own human nature, could be realized in the digital near future, where the only things left standing are a dead world exhausted of nature and one all-too-real virtual machine. The medium is the message more than ever before, for the digital information age promises a technological transformation of every aspect of reality, and us with it.

When Bill Gates speaks of the coming digital world, I am confident that most people know what he means. The digital technology of mobile phones, DVDs, personal digital assistants (PDAs), digital TV (DTV), and Sony PlayStations is ubiquitous enough that the reader will have taken at least a peek into the digital future.[2] The fact that you could be reading these words off a handheld illuminated screen speaks volumes about the changes currently taking place. Nevertheless, understanding that a digital age is in the making is very different from understanding the social and psychological implications of living in a digital age. This book stems from my belief that the meaning these changes will have for us is poorly understood today, and that gaining a greater understanding will require a critical questioning of some long and closely held assumptions.

Not least of these is the assumption that life will be better in the emerging digital dreamworld. Looking at the new digital you, what we actually see is a worsening of various social and psychological symptoms and the appearance of a whole host of new ones. In no particular order, these include the substitution of an always more alluring surrogate reality for social reality; the decline in the ability of everyday reality to provide people's lives with rich and lasting meaning, which coincides with the emptying of reality; the collapse of time and space that comes from living at the speed of electricity; the shrinking attention span that comes from living in a world filled with the clutter and clamor of a 24/7 society; the unfulfilled desire that comes with living in one reality while having our desires cultivated in another; the proliferation of technologies that mediate our experience, such that social interactions that were already mediated are now filtered through additional layers of artificial intelligence; the epidemic of people falling to every occasion, with new wireless gadgets allowing us to indulge every impulse; and the loss of memory and self-unity that results from living on the surface of reality, feeding off sugar-coated bits of fleeting information.

Rather than try to clarify each of these here, let me just give a few specifics to bring things into focus. As amazing as are inventions such as the Internet and wireless e-mail—allowing you to travel the world with your fingertips and reconnect with long-lost friends and family members—there is a darker side. Research has begun to show that jacking in to cyberspace is not necessarily going to help your overall social life, creating as it does in people greater feelings of isolation, loneliness, and depression. There is also growing evidence that by adding additional portals to virtual reality, we are supporting a general abandonment of the social and ecological world. This means that even if you are happily plugged in, or you do not plug in at all, you may nevertheless suffer as mainstream society goes digital.

Research also shows that the rise of the Internet and the proliferation of such things as digital cable have encouraged even greater passivity in people's lives, with America becoming a spectator nation. Pointing to this trend, public health researchers report that Americans experienced a dramatic rise in obesity in the 1990s, which led in turn to a significant increase in the most common form of diabetes. International epidemiological studies also suggest that the materialist ethos that drives our land of desire is making increasing numbers of people psychologically sick. As this has unfolded, many of us have gone from being reduced to consumers to being reduced to patients as well. This decline in mental health manifests itself in forms from depression to drug addiction (including alcohol addiction), to problems of hyperactivity and impulsivity (including attention deficit hyperactivity disorder, or ADHD), to problems of hostility and violence (for example, road rage and school violence), with drugs now appearing as panaceas for nearly every ailment from sexual dysfunction to social phobias. In all these categories, America is number one.

This is the look of the new digital you—the look of that free, unencumbered, wireless you, a you who wants not to be confronted with the here and now but rather distracted from it at all costs. In the old-fashioned, unplugged world, other people were extensions of ourselves, and we could not cope without them; in the emerging digital world, high technology is an extension of ourselves, and it seems we cannot cope without it.

Having suggested these trends, I must add that these are mostly side effects and symptoms, and they do not reveal what is really taking place behind the digital curtain. In taking a look behind it, as we do here, the questions raised and the tentative answers provided suggest a number of unsettling conclusions about the future of the future and our place in it. Among these is the conclusion that the modern period—*modernity*—has in large part been defined by an accelerating flight from reality to virtuality, especially in America. By this I mean that people's lives have moved away from the immediate world of the here and now—the unplugged world—and toward a more abstracted, artificial reality—the plugged-in world. The social philosopher Henri Lefebvre has described the result: "We are surrounded by emptiness, but it is an emptiness filled with signs."[3]

With the mind cultivated by the endless possibilities of a plugged-in reality, our lives have fallen into contradiction. We are increasingly torn between a fading reality that once provided lasting meaning and a digitally enhanced virtuality that reigns all powerful because it promises an escape from our growing sense of meaninglessness. With this abandonment well under way, the digital revolution marks an all-important shift from the modern to postmodern period—from modernity to *postmodernity*. This period has only just begun, however, and we are no more prepared to anticipate the coming changes than were those who lived on the edge of another time, when the world went modern.

More than anything else, the postmodern age will be a time when the very nature and meaning of reality fall into question, and us with them. Here we will see a further extraction of our lives from the slow and sensuous world of the here and now as we become fully interfaced with virtual worlds. We will also see a further blurring of what is natural versus what is artificial, as the capacity to take nature apart and rebuild it marches on. In short, we as a society are on the verge of stepping through to the other side of the looking glass, where the essence of nature—human nature included—is digitized into a data stream of zeroes and ones and downloaded into a virtual machine.

The coming digital world that Bill Gates and others promise will take us to a time that has, literally, no place. The name of this place-less place is *digitopia.*

DIGITALLY MASTERED

on the nature and meaning

of all that is digital

If going digital means big change, what does it mean to go digital? This question, which is the subject of this essay, is not as easy to answer as it might first appear. In order to understand the full implications of the digital revolution, we must look beyond its most obvious acronymous artifacts, including PCs, DTVs, CDs, PDAs, and DVDs.

As everyone knows, "digital" means a sharper image, a wireless connection, the magical realism of digital animation, clearer and more seamless sound, a tapeless tape recorder, a downloadable music track, a personal digital assistant, a filmless camera, an electronic pet, an instant message, stock tip, or news flash, and an always faster computer. Not all of this is good news. Digital technology permits a miniaturization of many technologies that can be quite insidious. Imagine being tagged with an inexpensive digital tracker that would allow anyone to track and record your motions without your knowing.[1] Imagine the uses of miniature video recorders. Such devices could be temporarily placed in a public rest room or your office, secretly recording such things as the keyboarding of computer passwords. Or imagine the digital information that comes with digital money, keys, identification, cameras, and so on. Anybody walking down the street can be investigated on the spot by the use of, among other digital equipment, an electronic and wireless fingerprint reader.[2]

When focusing on these new technologies, "digital" means several things. It means, first of all, just what electronic technology is supposed to mean: greater convenience, efficiency, portability, intelligence, memory, and affordability. It also means a continued expansion of the electronic frontier: greater speed in computing, various new movie projection technologies, improved Internet systems, and expanding satellite coverage are creating an ever-expanding and more realistic virtuality into which we can escape from both ourselves and others. Finally, it means the continued evolution of all media technologies that encourage the speeding up and globalizing of the world. We are at a critical juncture on an exponential curve of advancing technological change. Like the warp speed of *Star Trek*'s Starship *Enterprise,* this is the moment when every dimension of simulated reality will suddenly leap forward, leaving your old but already hyperdriven sense of reality behind.

As dramatic as all this may sound, it's only the beginning. Yes, "digital" means all of this, but it also means much more. In the most radical sense, the very idea of "digital" means deconstructing every aspect of reality into its most elementary parts, followed by a reconstruction of those parts into whatever postreality we might want—or at least whatever postreality certain groups, corporations, or nation-states might want. Although this reconstruction requires more than just the capacity to represent reality in the form of digital code, digitization is the central factor in the process. One reason is that the complexity involved in certain tasks—interactive video, human speech recognition, artificial intelligence, among others—can be handled only by the phenomenal processing speeds that digital technology allows. Generic algorithms are an example. Here the powers of supercomputing are used to simulate huge numbers of possible solutions to a well-defined problem. The problem ranges from drug development to mechanical engineering to artistic design, with the optimal solution being selected—in Darwinian fashion—as the computer applies a set of criteria to the rapidly generated output. This hyperaccelerated form of cultural evolution would not be possible without the supercomputing powers that digitization allows.

When viewed in this wider context, "digital" does not simply mean a quantitative improvement in the media technologies of the past, which include printing, radio, film, and television. Rather, it means that our cultural evolution has entered a new phase in its persistent quest to dominate every aspect of nature. Experiencing nature was not enough, so we sought to understand it. Understanding nature was not enough, so we seek to control it. Controlling nature was not enough, so we seek to enhance it. Enhancing nature was not enough, so we seek to reproduce it. Reproducing nature is not enough, so we seek to replace it. These are all human pursuits, but it's only through digitization that we are able, now, to take them to their ultimate conclusion.

This means that the rise of the "digital" will accelerate the tearing down of whatever distinction still remains today between what is real and what is simulated. As this tearing down takes place, the social and psychological effects of the digital revolution will become more apparent, as side effects, with you becoming all the more confused about who you are and what life you should lead. Is this film footage for real? Is this photo for real? Is this document for real? Is this money for real? Is this person I'm chatting with for real? Are my feelings for real? Is my desire for real? Am I for real? What is real?

From this radical perspective, the meaning of "digital" takes on a greater significance, implying as it does the supersession of our bricks-and-mortar reality with a plugged-in virtuality. Is this threat of a digital apocalypse for real, or is this just hype of an inverted kind? As I show, this is not some futuristic thought experiment, a nostalgic plea for "going Amish," or an apocalyptic science fiction fantasy. Nor is it an anticipation of things to come. For in many ways, the digital future is now.

At a time when the public is still coming to grips with the psychological impact of the analog world of television, people are suddenly facing an explosion of new imponderables raised by a rapidly expanding electronic world. One area of concern is the developing minds of young children. With still little consensus on how growing up watching television affects the moral sensibilities and behavioral impulses of children, parents and others are now confronting such questions in a much broader context that includes computers, the Internet, and video games. Digital technology thus represents change on two fronts: not only are there more portals into the world of make-believe, this alternative world is also becoming more hyper-realistic. Stephen Jay Gould makes the point with regard to another portal into virtuality, the IMAX theater:

> In this different threat to the intrinsically higher status of "real" objects, we can now make explicitly virtual representations so much bigger, so much scarier, so much more frenetic—in short, so much more viscerally thrilling in a primal physiological sense—that many people (as our kids do already) might come to prefer the virtual to the real. Why spend thousands of bucks to visit a tropical rain forest, trek and sweat in the heat, endure leech bites and Delhi belly, and see very few animals from very far away, when you can practically pet gargantuan-sized images on an IMAX screen for 10 bucks?[3]

Another example is Sony's new PlayStation 2. This multimedia device connects to the Web, plays DVDs, and, as a game console, brings interactive video together with high-definition, digitized images (at a cost to Sony of about $2.4 billion in development and production). While the original PlayStation of six or so years ago handled about 360,000 of the building blocks that produce real-time 3-D graphics—called polygons—per second, PlayStation 2 can run through between 20 million and 100 million a second.[4] The chip that serves as the centerpiece of the new PlayStation—Sony's "Emotion Engine"—is said to move data at about 48 gigabytes per second, compared to the 1.6 or so gigabytes of data per second handled by current PCs. Also, the graphic synthesizer necessary for the display of these graphics renders up to sixty frames and 75 million pixels a second, which is dramatically greater than for other state-of-the-art,

128-bit game consoles (e.g., the Sega Dreamcast renders only about 5 million pixels a second). Thus, for the PlayStation 2, "digital" means a 50- or 100-fold increase in processing power in a single upgrade in video technology—and you can be assured it won't be the last. Far from being a subject of pressing concern, this advancing digital wave of simulated reality raises questions that at a societal level we have yet to even ask.

Meanwhile, just how intense these experiences can be for mind and body became crystal clear in 1998, when hundreds of Japanese children experienced seizures after watching animation contained in a popular television cartoon.[5] While the American media covered the story, few if any journalists sensed its larger significance for a world that is becoming digitally mastered—a failure that I think follows from how journalists and the public dwell on content rather than on the medium as the message. Yet the overall message is a relatively simple one: with greater sophistication, intensity, and ubiquity, the plugged-in world inhabited by children and adults alike has a direct and profound effect on human consciousness. Asking the question "What happens to a generation immersed in the most violent, interactive entertainment ever created?" Paul Keegan writes in *Mother Jones* magazine:

Calling these experiences "games" understates their significance. They are closer to acid trips, altering your sense of perception in a fundamental way. Your stomach churns with motion sickness even though you're standing perfectly still. When you stop playing and stand up, objects in the room swim through space. The clock indicates you've been playing for an hour when you could swear it's been only 10 minutes. Later, driving down the highway, you feel like you are stopped in the middle of the road while cars around you slowly back up.[6]

As this example suggests, life in the digital world shapes the mind in its own image, such that the moods, rhythms, and images of the digital environment are rapidly becoming the dominant moods, rhythms, and images of the mental environment. This is something few seem to realize about mind and matter in these digital times: how you think and feel will go digital long before your brain and body do.

This brings us to an important conclusion about the nature and meaning of all that is "digital." It is the nature of change to occur gradually, and it's the nature of us humans to adapt to gradual change as it unfolds—the net result being that, even in these high-tech times, you are apt to view the digital revolution as representing nothing more than an incremental change in the existing nature of things, rather than what it really is: a quantum shift in the rendering of reality. And in some limited sense this is correct: digitization does indeed mean a continuation of certain changes that have long been taking place. The problem is that such incremental change should in no way be mistaken for insignificant change. After all, it was through incremental steps in biological evolution that both life and human beings came into being. It may also be through incremental steps of evolution—steps, that is, in our own cultural evolution—that human existence will cease, replaced by cybernetic existence instead.

Such a fantastic claim will no doubt strike some readers as just plain silly. That this is not the product of some overactive imagination, or some neoprimitivist conspiracy against the digitization of our world, was made clear enough in April 2000, when Bill Joy of Sun Microsystems published his oft-cited essay—in *Wired* magazine, no less—on our future in the technological future. The title of his essay was provocative: "Why the Future Doesn't Need Us."[7]

In his essay, Joy attempts to warn both policy makers and the public about the emerging threats posed by the technological rebuilding of nature and society through digitization and other related means. These range from biotechnology to a new atomic science called nanotechnology (both of which I discuss in later essays). In contrast to Joy's account, however, which suggests an eventual break in people's control over the machines that could build the future in their own image, the view taken here is that the future is already spinning out of control. As we shall see, Bill Joy expresses some valid concerns about where this technology could take us, but he fails to explore how these darker possibilities are rooted in the realities of today.

FOUR DNA BASES,
TWENTY-SIX LETTERS, A ZERO,
AND A ONE

how code continues to take over the world

In this essay I want to show that there is something inherent in the process of codification—in this case, the codification of reality through digitization—that gives it great transformative powers. Describing three instances of this codification process—geneticization, alphabetization, and digitization—I hope to show why the appearance of these particular processes will turn out to be the most pivotal moments in the history of our planet, and for the same reason: each represents a highly adaptive form of reproducible code that understands, organizes, and manipulates nature and reality from the bottom up. The greatest sources of complexity, it turns out, are drawn from elegant simplicity: four DNA bases, twenty-six letters, a zero, and a one.

With the possible exception of the physical chemistry that constitutes all the matter on Earth (and that has been codified in terms of the periodic table), the earliest instance of the power of codification dates back to the evolution of life on the planet. As first observed by scientists in 1943, the origins of life can be described as emerging from the organic compound deoxyribonucleic acid (DNA), which is found in the chromosomes of nearly all living cells. The full significance of this came ten years later, when James Watson and Francis Crick showed that the blueprints of life, contained in the DNA, actually consist of little more than successive combinations of four nucleotide bases: adenine, guanine, cytosine, and thymine. Specifically, the stuff of life was found to be a double-helix polymer composed of two spiraling DNA strands, each of which consists of a long chain of these four nucleotides. As the biologist Richard Dawkins puts it, "The river of genes is a digital river."[1] All this seemed quite impressive at the time and still does, especially when we consider the complexity of species such as our own, not to mention the fact that variations in the sequence of these bases have led to millions of different species of plants and animals. In human terms, as another biologist put it, "the text is three billion years old, has six billion copies in print, runs three billion letters long . . . , and is written entirely in four characters (A, T, C, G) with no spaces or punctuation. The book, of course, is a great classic, The Sequence of the Human Genome."[2]

The second and equally remarkable instance of codification came about much later, with alphabetization. Today we take our twenty-six-letter alphabet for granted and think of it as a "natural" part of our world. In truth, the shift from the fleeting sounds of *oral* cultures to the fixed symbols of *literal* ones was very much the result of an invention—the twenty-two-letter Semitic alphabet—and it rivals, both in importance and in effect, the evolution of genetic code.

Written language is often associated with the rise of complex social systems and the emergence of modern industrial societies. However, the emphasis is usually placed on the invention of the printing press, because of its revolutionary impact in ushering in the modern age. This is an understandable emphasis in that the publishing of mass numbers of copies of different texts eventually brought widespread literacy to much of the world. Nevertheless, the advent of the printing press was but a small step once spoken languages were converted to code by transforming sound into bits of information (called letters).[3] In fact, unlike movable-type printing, which was invented more than once, all alphabets derive from the same Semitic alphabet, dating back to 2000 B.C.

The codified nature of writing (and history), which parallels the codified nature of biology (and life), can be seen when we compare alphabetic and ideographic systems of writing (the latter of which are still used today by the Chinese, among others). Both these language systems represent a reduction of oral language into signs, although only the former reduces language into a basic information code (the latter relies on a separate symbol for each word or idea). Like the biological system of four DNA bases, a system of language that relies on only a small set of interchangeable units has an unmistakable power above all others. Some of these advantages are simple, such as the ease of transferring the alphabet to a keyboard, while others are rather difficult to conceptualize. To give an example of the latter, Eric Havelock argues in his *Origins of Western Literacy* that the rise of analytical thought by ancient Greeks came about through the introduction of vowels into the Semitic alphabet.[4] Havelock posits that this contribution increased the abstraction of language, allowing in turn a further abstraction in thought (by "abstraction" I mean that the source of experience is not direct or unmediated with regard to the unplugged world).[5]

While the quasi-pictographic language of Chinese is the most complex system of symbols in the world, it is by no means the most powerful. In fact, for better or worse, this amount of complexity at "code level" hinders the capacity of the system to reach the level of abstracted "information" attained through alphabetic languages. For this reason, as Walter Ong notes in his classic study of written languages, *Orality and Literacy,* "There can be no doubt that the [Chinese] characters will be replaced by the roman alphabet as soon as all the people in the People's Republic of China master the same Chinese language . . . , the Mandarin now being taught everywhere. The loss to literature will be enormous, but not so enormous as a Chinese typewriter using over 40,000 characters."[6]

If natural history came from a system of codification involving a few nucleotides and human history came from a system of codification involving a few symbolic characters, what will come of our current fascination with the machine language of zeros and ones? As much as we cannot help but be aware of the coming digital age, the long-range implications of the digitization process are either unappreciated or, as in the case of its proponents, blurred by romanticization. As geneticization and alphabetization would suggest, digitization not only has the power to reproduce that which it represents, it also has the power to do this in a highly efficient, stable, and indefinite (if not infinite) manner.

Like DNA and the Roman alphabet, digital code operates on discrete units of representation that can be reproduced with little or no error.[7] This is unlike analog representations of reality, which rely not on discrete codes but on continuous waves or fluctuations in energy. Because the latter has variability (error) inherent in its reproduction, there is a loss or distortion of information that occurs each time the analog signal is reproduced. In contrast, by converting reality into discrete, unitary bits of digital information, we can reproduce it ad infinitum. Also, with reality represented as discrete bits, we can use digitization to reconstruct reality from the bottom up. It is not a great exaggeration to say that digitization puts reality in our hands to do with as we please. When combined with other technologies, the result is that we are approaching a moment in history that, in terms of the discrepancy between real knowledge and total power, parallels the advent of the atomic age. We have the power to tinker with the very building blocks of the animate and inanimate world, but we have little or no knowledge of what this will mean for our future, and for the future of our planet.

Of course, the implications of all this depend entirely on what is digitized in the first place and how we manipulate it once it is. When it's a music track on a CD, it's the recording of live music that can be manipulated. When it's a photo of a person placed on the cover of a magazine, it's the representation of that person that can be manipulated. When it's a familiar voice on the other end of a telephone line, it's the identity of another person that can be manipulated. When it's the face of the woman next door, it's the look of a real human being that can be manipulated. When it's the genetic structure of a virus or a plant, it's the nature of life that can be manipulated. When it's the neuroanatomical organization of a human brain, it's a human mind that can be manipulated.

While some of these examples may sound like science fiction, it's useful to note that only thirty years ago it all sounded like science fiction. It is also useful to note that billions of dollars are currently being spent each year on technologies for decoding and reconstructing reality, some of which are already available. The obvious examples involve music and video (including Sony's PlayStation 2), but this is also taking place in realms such as speech recognition, reconstructive surgery, and biotechnology.

Digitization is also making great gains in its capacity to reproduce nature and reality by joining forces with the other systems of code. In the case of alphabetization, it's clear that more complex computer programs will continue to be developed to analyze the meaning of speech and written language; there will also be advances in artificial intelligence. This will immediately improve, among other things, the efficiency and accuracy of search engines, grammar checkers, and voice recognizers. And we should not overlook the more immediate example: one could not download and read this book using digital technology were it not for the fact that alphabetization lends itself perfectly to digitization.

As for genetic code, we have recently witnessed the early success of the Human Genome Project in "breaking" the human genetic code, a project that was transformed when a private company, Celera Genomics, took most of the deciphering process out of the hands of scientists and turned it over to machines.[8] Having succeeded in converting genetic code into digital code, scientists from public and private institutions can now access this code—Celera's "bioinformatics products"—for research purposes via the Web. Where this will take us nobody knows, and few seem to realize the God-like implications of decoding the mystery of life and then downloading it into machines.

For if genetic code can be turned into sequences of DNA bases, and if sequences of these bases can in turn be translated into digital streams of zeros and ones, it's clear that *being human* can itself be reduced to *being digital.*

THE ONE AND ONLY REALITY

not appreciating what reality really is,

we have squandered its substance and materiality

Just as there can be no progress in discussing our long journey into digitopia without first considering the meaning of all that is "digital," neither can there be any progress without considering the meaning and nature of what we call "reality." Although I wish to raise doubts about the viability of a digital dreamworld that would satisfy your basic psychological needs (i.e., digitopia), I am more than willing to confess at the outset that it's far too late to go hunting for some pure primitive reality into which you can return. In fact, reality is already so shot through with virtuality that the question is not one of real versus virtual but one of just how virtual you wish to be.

Of course, none of this makes any sense as long as you hold on to the idea that there are in fact two separable worlds: the world of material reality and the world of virtual reality. According to this common but archaic view, you are in either one world or the other, and as long as you can see the sky above and the ground below you are still grounded in the material, corporeal world. By contrast, when you look at how the images, rhythms, and desires of the plugged-in world are showing up as durable needs and expectations in the un-plugged world, you can see that these two worlds are in fact over-lapping ones, with the first gradually eclipsing the second. If the desire for distraction has pushed your family dinner in front of the television, or if your desire for new e-mail has punctured the tranquillity of your day off, this applies to you.

Anyone who has seen the popular 1999 film *The Matrix* has some idea of where our unbridled pursuit of digitopia could eventually take us.[1] With its digital collage of high-definition graphics, intense action sequences, and explosive Dolby sound, *The Matrix* introduces audiences to an e-world in which people live out a wholly digital existence. Because being jacked in to the matrix induces in the brain a neurophysiological and phenomenological experience identical to that produced by everyday material reality, it turns out that the inhabitants of this world do not realize that they are actually living out their existence as brains in a vat, prisoners of the virtual machine. To escape from the matrix, people must first become aware of its existence, and so all are lying in wait for a cybersavior—Keanu Reeves, perhaps?—to reveal not the man but the machine behind the curtain.

All this is great fun, yes, a first-rate science fiction film. And while it is tempting to view *The Matrix* as a futuristic fantasy prophesying a holy war between ourselves and sentient robots, the film actually provides a powerful allegory for the present day. The matrix of *The Matrix* is an all-encompassing virtual world in which artificiality has achieved the full status of earthly reality, and with essentially no recognition by those who live in it. The allegorical nature of the film thus lies in the fact that much the same supersession of reality by virtuality is unfolding in America today. Indeed, one wonders how many people, while interfaced with the big screen, had any awareness that they were watching *The Matrix* in a matrix.

People are not yet brains in a vat. But we are increasingly a people who live a virtual existence yet have little or no awareness of just how virtual our existence is. Our time is increasingly spent in artificial worlds of computer cyberspace and video games. People's needs and wants are increasingly shaped by cinematic emotions and images. And our inflated aspirations for our own personalized futures are increasingly reflective of television and all its commercial possibilities. In other words, even if the digital revolution were brought to a halt today, millions of people would remain caught in an existential limbo, torn between the artificial dreams of simulated reality and the old-fashioned world in which they try to live them out. Put simply, should a true digitopia ever come into existence, it's unlikely you would ever remember the moment you first stepped into it.

Reality and virtuality are not as separable in our lives as we'd like to believe—and are even less so with each passing day. In fact, a process of virtualization that subrogates reality right in front of our eyes has long been under way. We fail to recognize this process, however, because we naturally accommodate the virtual as real, immediately forgetting each surface of reality as it is washed away. I realize it sounds absurd to suggest that reality is not what you think it is, for if there's anything one knows through and through it should be reality. In truth, reality turns out to be quite a slippery subject.

In its most basic sense, the concept of "reality" refers to the idea of an absolute foundation or "bedrock" of experience. Is it real or is it Memorex? But even here we have a problem, for decades of social science research have shown that the mind has a great capacity—a fundamental capacity, I believe—to revise and re-revise what counts as fundamental reality. Despite three centuries of philosophical effort to prove otherwise, the mind seems more interested in making sense of the world, whatever world that might be, than it does in holding on to some primordial reality that is no longer visible or viable.

Imagine if you were given a pair of strange-looking glasses and asked to wear them continuously during your waking hours for several days. Suppose these glasses had lenses shaped so that all vertical lines (e.g., the edges of walls and buildings) looked somewhat curved. Naturally, when you first don these glasses you see a world somewhat bent out of shape. A question that arises is what, if anything, would happen to your vision with the passage of time. Fortunately, we know the answer to this question, since this and similar psychological tests of perception have been conducted for several decades.[2] So what happens? As the psychologist James Gibson showed in his pathbreaking research on the "ecological" nature of perception, the mind actually adapts to such distortions, such that the person eventually comes to see the curved lines as straight ones. Just as surprising is the fact that when the glasses are finally removed, following the adaptation process, the person sees straight lines as curved lines for a short time, curved the opposite direction from when they first put on the glasses (these lines are called afterimages or aftereffects).

In one sense, the main finding of Gibson's study suggests the mind's capacity to filter out distortions and find its way back to a true reality. After all, the lines out there in the "real world" are in fact straight ones. But this getting back to the truth also shows the mind's willingness to ignore immediate reality in favor of another, more pressing one. Since your awareness of the world derives from direct sensory experience, it's surprising that, with the glasses on, the mind actually comes to override the experience of seeing what is actually on the backs of your eyeballs: curved lines! And as we shall see, this is just the point. Your sense of reality derives from much more than your immediate, direct experience; it derives from your cumulative experience, with the logical goal of adapting to whatever reality you happen to inhabit, whether earthly or synthetic, real or virtual, moral or amoral. This presents a daunting challenge in trying to hold on to "reality" as we enter the digital age, as the mind continues to adapt to simulated worlds that are ever more real than reality itself.

More real than reality itself? Indeed. Not only is this possible, it's in fact the reason why you can live a virtual existence yet have little or no awareness of just how virtual your existence is. As the historian Daniel Boorstin noted four decades ago, we now live in a "world where fantasy is more real than reality" such that "we risk being the first people in history to have been able to make their illusions so vivid, so persuasive, so 'realistic' that they can live in them."[3]

Not long ago I was watching the 1986 Michael Mann film *Manhunter* (this film is based on author Thomas Harris's *Red Dragon,* the predecessor to *The Silence of the Lambs*). In one unremarkable scene, the main character—a man who works as a criminal profiler for the FBI—is talking on the phone in an empty room of a house. What I noticed about this scene was that the sound quality was poor—it sounded coarse and hollow—and certainly not near the quality of contemporary big-budget films, such as Mann's more recent film *The Insider* (the wedding scene in Arthur Hiller's 1970 classic *Love Story* provides very much the same example). What I noticed just a moment later was more interesting. While the sound of the lead character talking on the phone seemed less than realistic, it was in fact very close to what a voice should sound like in the vacant room of a house. Why, then, did it not *sound* real? The reason makes the point: it did not sound real because my sense of what "real" should sound like has been conditioned by the "unreality" of more recent films, where everything is—and must be—more real than reality itself. Had I been watching *Manhunter* when it first came out, in 1986, my guess is that the sound quality in this scene would have passed me by as altogether "real."

The general implication of this inflationary process is that good old-fashioned reality cannot stand up against the realities perfected by virtual technologies. Most films are likely to become dated for this reason, not just because the clothing and language have fallen out of fashion but also because the realism presented in the film does not pass for reality any longer. This is aptly captured in the following remark, which is taken from an interview with Phil Tippett, a film animator who helped create the dinosaurs seen in *Jurassic Park:*

Everything changed overnight with *Jurassic Park.* I like to use the example of the 1925 fantasy film *Lost World,* which was about an expedition to South America to bring back prehistoric animals. It was created using the stop-frame technology—the most advanced, most sophisticated use of the process at that time! If you read the reviews of *Lost World,* the critics back then were ecstatic—they couldn't believe it! They thought the filmmakers must have gone into the South American plateaus to shoot real dinosaurs! My kids watch the movie today and say "My God!—it looks like they were made of papier-mâché and clay!"[4]

This realization would hardly be earth-shattering if it all started and ended with motion pictures. But when the process of digital perfection spills over into everyday behavior and experience, we begin to see how it overshadows all earthly realities, creating a sense of expectation that cannot be met easily, if at all, in what remains of the unplugged world. Indeed, the question arises as to where exactly the arbiters of reality—corporate media, the movie industry, advertisers, writers of popular fiction, and so forth—plan to take it. On this theme I cannot imagine a more striking example than how corporate culture manufactures our society's beauty standards, especially for women.

For some time now, girls in America have been growing up in a culture of perfection where what passes as reality has become toxic. Today this culture of perfection is going digital, such that not only can the slightest "imperfections" be cleaned up, an entire object of desire can be constructed out of bits and pieces of humanity. In the abstract, the claim that virtual worlds make the mind in their own image might seem hyperbolic and playful. In the case of the beauty myth, however, we see just how "real" it can become. Young women have millions of exemplars from which to judge the normal sizes and shapes of the female body, yet this vast pool of reality is somehow overridden by a narrow band of hyperreality. As with the case of motion pictures, the preponderance of hyperreal exemplars has the effect of turning back and distorting your sense of everyday reality. "I haven't looked thirty since I was twenty," quips a model in an episode of *Law and Order.*

Note that this matches perfectly the finding of Gibson's study above. The mind's willingness to ignore immediate reality in favor of another, more pressing one is exactly what a young woman faces. In fact, when researchers have assessed women's own body images, they have found this same phenomenon.[5] When faced with their own image, what appears on the back of their retinas is not what is seen; rather, young women often see a "fatter" image. Note, however, that when faced with the same body image morphed onto another face, they show no such distortions. Again, people's sense of reality derives from much more than their immediate, direct experience; it derives from cumulative experience with the logical goal of adapting to whatever pressing reality one inhabits. Unfortunately, for many women, this reality happens to make them sick.

In Part III of the book we shall look more closely at this capacity of virtualized images to define our standards of reality, which in turn creates a lust for virtual impossibilities. Here I simply want to conclude with the more basic point: there is no reason for us to believe that what looks, feels, or sounds like "the real thing" is anything more than a simulated construct that, through its ubiquity and privileged status in our flickering society, has forced its way onto the stage of reality.

THE REAL AND THE TRUE

how the academics' debate over objectivity

and truth missed the point

We live in self-imposed exile from communal conversation and action. The public square is naked. American politics has lost its soul. The republic has become procedural, and we have become unencumbered selves. Individualism has become cancerous. We live in an age of narcissism and pursue loneliness. These expressions are alarming not because they predict the ruin of the state. . . . Rather, these expressions of distress should disquiet us because they indicate that we have no common life, that what holds us all together is a cold and impersonal design.

Albert Borgmann[1]

These words from Albert Borgmann's *Crossing the Postmodern Divide* describe the present situation in contemporary America. This is a situation that has led not only to widespread dissatisfaction, psychopathology, antisocial behavior, and massive use of psychotropic drugs, but also to a crisis in meaning. A world emptied of meaning leaves you in despair about what to do with your life and how to restore meaning in a fragmented, hurried, and harried society. It also leaves you confused about what is true, how to determine what is right and wrong, and whether truth and morality really exist in any absolute sense. While both of these aspects of meaning are dealt with in this book, it's the latter that I wish to address in this essay.

In October 2000, *Forbes ASAP*—the digital magazine of the Forbes media empire—published its fifth annual "big issue," asking what is true in the age of the Internet.[2] With dozens of essays by a host of authors, celebrities, inventors, CEOs, and others, the answer to the question was found not in any one essay but in the essays as a whole. At least in my reading, it was clear throughout that "truth" was something people were quick to give up, to the extent that the question of truth was examined at all. With all this ambivalence, it wasn't easy to find many writers who were willing to tell what seemed to me to be the only obvious truth; namely, that in the age of the Internet, "what is true" has fallen into as much fragmentation and abstraction as has the world to which truth is meant to apply.

Given this, it should be no surprise that there is also a debate raging over the possibility of "truth" in the academy. What I am referring to is the continuing debate over "postmodernism." Here, as in the special issue of *Forbes ASAP,* the crisis of meaning in contemporary life has led to a struggle over the meaning and nature of truth and whether the reality of today is substantial enough that objectivity and truth can prevail.

The term "postmodernism" has many meanings, but the one that has attracted the greatest controversy in recent years involves epistemology. This deals with the division between relative subjectivity versus objective truth, or what is also known as the territorial debate between the modernist realists (usually housed in the sciences) and the postmodernist relativists (usually housed in the social sciences and the humanities). The debate is territorial because, to the extent that postmodernism is persuasive in the academy, the sciences are weakened in their claim of having special access to universal truths. If postmodernism is a hoax, on the other hand, the humanities lose their claim to deconstructing science and the sciences are put back onto a firm epistemological foundation. Of course, the game of what is the truth about truth is won not by proving what is true, as this is logically impossible in a war over the nature of truth. Rather, the game is won by attaining the power to declare what is true. Even in the postmodernists' world, truth is power and power is truth.

To continue with this, note that "soft" postmodernists associate themselves with a school by another name, called "social constructionism," while "hard" postmodernists are just that, postmodernists. Those in the former group are likely to argue that a real world exists, that there are facts you can know about this world, but that your understanding needs always to be scrutinized for how personal and cultural history has influenced your interpretation of those facts. The other, more controversial group is likely to argue that the historical and social realms have such a determining influence over your ways of knowing that it makes little difference whether or not any real world exists, since you can never escape your own matrix of understanding. Incidentally, I would locate myself and the ideas expressed here as clearly in the former, social-constructionist camp.

The "postmodernism" debate is tangled up with multiculturalism and feminism as well, with many of the same issues at stake. The most important of these involves a questioning of the universality of truth put forward by the "dominant groups" of culture, both past and present. If cultural and personal experiences fundamentally shape the way you understand the world (as feminists have argued with respect to gender and people of color have argued with respect to race), the question arises as to whether knowledge is always conditional to those who hold it. Naturally, the answer to this question has great implications, from possible racial biases in college curricula and standardized testing to gender bias in medical research.

The reason I have focused on this issue can at this point be made clear. I think there is an underlying problem with the form this debate has taken thus far, one that relates directly to the nature of reality in the digital world. As the substance of reality has been transformed by media and other technologies and your life falls into greater abstraction, the relationship between truth and reality has become all the more tenuous. And because there is an important relationship between the nature of reality and your capacity to unearth truths about it, it makes no sense that the debate be focused on the isolated and absolute question of whether one can know universal truths. Instead, it should be redirected to the more dynamic and historical question of whether truth can survive in the abstraction and fragmentation of the postmodern world, especially truth as you confront it every day as a public citizen participating in a democratic society.

Said another way, if for thousands of years technology has been used increasingly to mediate our experience of the material world, then is not the current crisis over knowledge and truth itself a product of our own ongoing cultural evolution, which pushes us further into abstraction, complexity, and confusion? If in these digital times our connection to the social and ecological world is being rapidly redirected to a growing number of electronic portals leading into virtual space, would it not also be true that the digital age will only fan the fires of the postmodern debate, raising even greater questions about the nature of reality and our place in it? If relativism is becoming the dominant outlook today, perhaps the reason is that we are drifting away from a shared social reality rooted in social and ecological necessities. With the supersession of shared reality by simulated reality, can it be any surprise that objectivity and truth have lost their power in contemporary society, where questions of truth now divide rather than unite?

Looked at in this way, *Forbes ASAP* asked the wrong question. Before we can know "what is true," we must first know what is "reality" and what is the relationship between "the real" and "the true."

However paradoxical it may seem in the information age, a greater understanding of nature has translated into more complexity rather than less. Possessing more information does not necessarily mean understanding more. By making the world an exponentially more complex place and by being more interested in the world's problems than any real, permanent solutions to them—from starvation to war to ignorance to poverty to psychological dysfunction—

we have promoted an escalation of information and cultural change that threatens our very capacity to make sense of, and have any kind of control over, the world.

Moral relativism is one of the most obvious results, as are some of the avenues people have taken to overcome it, including religious fundamentalism. In the United States, moral relativism is blamed on various cultural trends, from divorce to Hollywood films. But this view is too narrow. The larger issue is how impossible and irrelevant absolute morality is in a world saturated in an ever-changing hyper-reality. When a thousand points of light shine upon you in a commercial war over your thoughts, feelings, and wants, truth and clarity of mind don't stand a chance. This is partly because the message is mixed. But even more important is the fact that the root source of your knowledge is no longer necessarily tied to direct experience in a vibrant sphere of tradition and culture. Social communities have become less cohesive and relationships more impersonal; as a consequence, knowledge is increasingly removed from direct experience in the world.[3] This has allowed mass media to acquire a much greater control over the images and ideas that come to define your sense of yourself and the world.

As the technological mediation of people's experience continues to expand in the digital age, we should expect the current crisis over objectivity and truth to become even more paramount. For this reason, the debate over moral relativism, truth, and "postmodernism" should be refocused on how our continued journey into hyperculture increases the gap between what is real and what is true. As this continues, it will become increasingly clear why the digital revolution is making the very meaning of reality the most pressing social question of our day.

SURVIVING *SURVIVOR*

how to survive when lost

between virtual reality and real virtuality

I have said much about the nature of reality and how it will continue to be transformed through our unbridled pursuit of digitopia. There is an important aspect of this transformation that has yet to be spelled out, however.

We live in a world that privileges image and illusion over substance and depth. The matrix of images and illusions operates today on two highly advanced fronts. We have already begun to discuss the first, how the world of virtuality shapes your mind in its own image, leaving you increasingly dazed and confused in what's left of the unplugged world. The second refers not to these virtual worlds but to the reality that is trying to compete with them. This is the story of a stage within a stage, with the stage on which you take up the roles of everyday life being "upstaged" by what takes place on a more dramatic—and plugged-in—secondary stage. The former was described by Lewis Mumford in 1964 as follows:

In his earthly theater man is by turns architect and scenic designer, director and stagehand, playwright and spectator; and above all he is an actor whose whole life is "such stuff as dreams are made on." Yet he is so formed and shaped by the nature of the stage, by the roles that he assumes, by the plots that he superimposes, that every aspect of the drama has substance and takes on some measure of significance.[1]

What we have here is the continued dramatization of the unplugged world, which follows like a shadow in pursuit of the always more amplified plugged-in world. As Neal Gabler shows in *Life the Movie,* the result is that life itself has become a zone of perpetual entertainment. "Acting as an Ebola virus," he writes, "entertainment has even invaded organisms no one would ever have imagined could provide amusement." Entertainment has become a source of escape from reality, while reality has been banalized into a twenty-four-hour-a-day escape from itself.

Thus, at the very moment when virtuality is becoming more real—a process to be forever advanced through digitization—the real world is also becoming more virtual. In one noted example, then vice presidential candidate Dan Quayle found himself in what seemed like a real-life debate over "family values," except that it was with a television character: Murphy Brown. In a more recent example, in the wake of the first successful run of *Survivor,* the NBC *Today* show booked Dawn Wells, who played Mary Ann on *Gilligan's Island,* to talk about it. Joel Stein, writing in *Time,* did not miss the significance of the moment, noting that it was "a fake person analyzing a fake event." To this he adds, "reporters were having trouble distinguishing the results of a four-month old, prerecorded television show from actual live news. CBS cast its local-news anchors in a deserted island set with tiki torches. And because CBS's news shows could monopolize the newsmakers created by its entertainment division, the other networks had to be pretty creative in coming up with folks to talk about the CBS show." This is obviously where Dawn Wells came in.

The implication is that, with the hyperreal and the surreal closing in on both sides, with one reflecting off the other, we are being sealed, however unknowingly or unwittingly, within a virtual house of mirrors. In the meantime, with our connection to reality becoming "unhinged by simulation," it is becoming less and less clear what side of reality we're on.[2] "We are in possession of all the information," writes the French social theorist Jean Baudrillard. "We are no longer spectators, but actors in the performance, and actors increasingly integrated into the course of that performance. Whereas we could face up to the unreality of the world as spectacle, we are defenceless before the extreme reality of this world, before this virtual perfection."[3] To some, I suppose, this sounds wonderful—a world of perpetual fun. But to anyone who believes that a rich and meaningful life can come only from a deep engagement in an enduring social and physical world, this can only sound like disaster. For in such an all-encompassing virtuality, everything becomes surface, with no depth.

I will distinguish here between these two trends by referring to the hyperreal as *virtual reality*—as I have been doing thus far—and the surreal as *real virtuality*. Real virtuality and virtual reality lead to the same place, total virtuality (cast here in the metaphor of digitopia), but it should be remembered that one pushes while the other pulls. Let me give some examples.

Consider, for starters, popular TV programs such as *Who Wants to Be a Millionaire* and *Survivor*. Reality programs such as these provide the clearest picture of how the gap between virtual reality and real virtuality is closing. On the one hand, these programs are just that, intensively produced television programs. On the other, the celebrities who come out of them are not well-known actors; in fact, they are not paid actors at all, they are just regular people like you and me. So from the viewer's point of view, is this virtual reality or real virtuality? It's both. It's real virtuality in the sense that everyday people are incorporated into a program to engage more or less in whatever behavior they choose—that is, it's more or less real. However, it's also virtual reality in the sense that it presents a world of artificial possibilities that are for all practical purposes out of this world. After all, as "real" as these programs are for those involved in them, most of us are not going to make it onto the program, nor are we going to become rich or famous, even if we do.

Of course this is the very reason why digitopia looms so large on the digital horizon. As a customized dreamworld where all ambitions can be realized at will, real virtuality is no longer just life lived as a perpetual game to be watched, it's life lived as a perpetual game to be played. Sherry Turkle describes an early precursor of such a world, which is an interactive computer game of "intergalactic exploration and wars" based partly on the television program *Star Trek: The Next Generation.*[4] Noting the thousands of players who each spend up to eighty hours a week engaged in this world of make-believe, Turkle describes one player who says, "This is more real than my real life." It turns out that this player was actually a man playing as a woman pretending to be a man. While I personally cannot imagine anything more dull than being an all-powerful celebrity in a virtual world made for one, examples such as this have convinced me that if such a virtual paradise were built, millions would come.

But let's get back to the matter at hand. Shows such as *Millionaire* and *Survivor* are not the only examples of how the walls between real virtuality and virtual reality are closing in. While most viewers see films such as *The Truman Show* and *EdTV* as just more entertainment, they actually represent something unique in the world of hyperculture. In a traditional film, you are asked to "suspend reality" in order to imagine that the events taking place are real ones, even though they are not. In films such as *The Truman Show* and *EdTV,* however, you are asked to go one step further, pretending that you are a voyeur watching real life trapped on the screen. In other words, these films present you with a virtual-reality version of real virtuality. As this is too confusing a situation even for the digital self to make sense of, we are fortunate that the situation has since been simplified. That is, we now have various "real-life" equivalents showing up, such as *Big Brother.* These programs are not as visually or dramatically impressive as their virtual-reality equivalents—after all, they're real, not hyperreal—but they seem to offer enough real virtuality that people still want to watch.

Let me summarize the situation just to make sure I've made it as complicated and confusing as it really is. We begin in life with everyday real life in our face, independent of film. In the old days this simply meant living, although today it also seems to require a lot of acting and self-fashioning as well, at least for some. Next, there is real life captured on film and presented to you as just that. This is called a documentary. After this there are films with paid actors in fictional or true stories. Sometimes these films are done in a documentary style to make it appear as though they are more than just films, although usually they are done in more dramatic fashion in which the film looks and feels more real, or hyperreal. Next, there are films in which the actors are acting as real people who do or do not know that, within the story of the film, they are actually on film (e.g., *EdTV* and *The Truman Show*). Going one step further, we find programs containing real people who not only are acting as real people, but who actually are (e.g., *Big Brother, Survivor*).

Actually, this is not the final intermingling of real virtuality and virtual reality. This would be the end of film altogether, with all of us acting as actors on a digital stage that needs no film because there is no longer anything beyond the film. This is the stage I've called *digitopia*.

DIGITAL MECHANICS

measuring the impact of the digital revolution

In Dave Grossman's book *On Killing: The Psychological Cost of Learning to Kill in War and Society,* he describes how during World War II soldiers frequently failed to fire their weapons in combat situations, a problem that had also been identified in earlier wars, including the American Civil War.[1] By comparison, Grossman tells us, firing rates were much improved by the time of the Vietnam War (up from about 15 to 20 percent to about 90 to 95 percent) and had been moderately improved at the time of the Korean war (55 percent). Why did soldiers' willingness to fire their rifles to kill other human beings suddenly change after centuries of noncompliance? And, perhaps more important for our purposes, what does this have to do with the look of the new digital you? As it turns out, these questions bring the same answer.

Grossman, a retired lieutenant colonel Army Ranger who was also a professor at West Point, reports in *On Killing* that the recent shift in firing rates in combat situations was the result of new methods developed by the military (and by law enforcement agencies) for desensitizing individuals to the violence of killing. These methods consist of applying classic desensitization techniques, in which individuals are asked to repeatedly simulate the act of killing in multiple contexts, thereby gradually replacing voluntary responses with involuntary reflexes. In essence, the act of killing becomes more probable because it no longer requires a conscious human decision. As a result, desensitization techniques reduce what Grossman describes as people's natural reluctance to kill.

So how does this apply to the subject at hand? It applies because, as Grossman himself shows, the contexts of simulation in which desensitization takes place have been replicated within a large variety of action-oriented media, especially interactive video games. The goal in the latter case is not to create killers but rather to create action, although the different motives seem not to change the effect. What Grossman argues specifically is that, in creating video technology that simulates the act of killing thousands of times, we are subjecting children to the same desensitization that soldiers experience. The result: you now live in a society in which hundreds of thousands of children have had their natural "safety catch" removed. Kids are not natural-born killers, Grossman tells us, but they can be primed for killing.

Having said this, let me make it clear that neither Grossman nor I believe that, in having this safety catch removed, kids are now destined to become killers. This brings me to the subject of this essay. Whether it's the content of video games, television, or film, whether it's the frenetic and high-speed graphics that come with greater digitization, whether it's the increasing realism that's available because of new digital technologies, or whether it's the ever-expanding technological mediation of your connections to the social and ecological world, the impact of media and their messages on the life of the mind is complex, cumulative, and multifaceted—and it will never be as simple as a one-to-one cause-and-effect relationship. With regard to the particular effect of media violence on violent behavior in children, Grossman explains:

> Another way to look at this is to make an analogy with AIDS. AIDS does not kill people; it simply destroys the immune system

and makes the victim vulnerable to death by other factors. The "violence immune system" exists in the midbrain, and conditioning in the media creates an "acquired deficiency" in this immune system. With this weakened immune system, the victim becomes more vulnerable to violence-enabling factors, such as poverty, discrimination, drug addiction (which can provide powerful motives for crimes in order to fulfill real or perceived needs), or guns and gangs (which can provide the means and "support structure" to commit violent acts).[2]

As Grossman suggests, there can be no doubt that the content of video games has a negative impact on some children and adolescents by dramatically lowering the trigger-pressure threshold that must be reached before an act of violence will occur. Let me give an example. Only a few days before writing this I read a newspaper account of five teenagers from "solidly middle-class families" who lured a delivery boy into a dark alley and killed him for a $60 meal.[3] One of the teenagers involved, the only female, was said to have been "at home much of Friday, listening to CD's—hip hop and Spanish music—writing e-mail messages, watching television. About 5 P.M. she told her grandmother she was going over to Mr. Tyson's house. . . . [The grandmother] said that about 9 P.M., she beeped her granddaughter, who called her back on the cell phone [her grandmother] had bought for her a few months ago." According to the article, this same cell phone was used by the girl later in the evening to lure the delivery boy into the hands of her male friends, who killed him just prior to midnight. The point is not to blame this death on video games or video-game technology, but rather to remind the reader just how low the threshold for killing has become. In this particular instance, at least according to the initial report, the threshold appears to be reached with little more than a case of Friday-night boredom.

And who knows, maybe a history of playing video games, combined with all the other media exposure kids experience today, did play a significant role in this killing. When the American Psychiatric

Association, the National Institute of Mental Health (NIMH), and the American Medical Association (AMA) each separately studied this issue with regard to the realm of television (which is not even interactive), all found a conclusive link between violent images and violent behavior.[4] The American Psychiatric Association report summarizes, "Over the last three decades, the one overriding finding in research on the mass media is that exposure to media portrayals of violence increases aggressive behaviors." It also notes that, at least before the appearance of the Internet, "the typical American child watches 28 hours of television a week, and by the age of 18 will have seen 16,000 simulated murders and 200,000 acts of violence. . . . Commercial television for children is 50–60 times more violent than prime-time programs for adults, as some cartoons average more than 80 violent acts per hour."

Buttressing this latter finding, a recent report by the Federal Trade Commission (September 11, 2000) found "pervasive and aggressive marketing" of restricted films and video games to children.[5] According to the report, the most popular restricted movies, music, and video games are regularly marketed to children as young as twelve. In one memorandum cited in the report, flyers and posters for R-rated movies were to be distributed to kids in organizations such as Camp Fire Boys and Girls.[6] Not only does this point to the mass exposure of young children to explicit images, it also suggests that such exposure is viewed by the industry, in Joe Camel–like fashion, as an effective way of conditioning a thirst for explicit images in individuals. If it weren't, why would advertising be going to kids this young? Of course, this pattern is exactly what Dave Grossman documents in his book. He reports that, corresponding with the increase in violence in the media, violence in Western countries has increased dramatically since 1977.

Meanwhile, those who raise questions about the transformative effects of being plugged in, whether on children or on adults, continue to be criticized by others who rely on the cartoon notion of causation described above. For example, an article in *The Washington Post* cites a vice president of a video-game company as suggesting that if violent games bred violent people, our prisons would be full of video-game players.[7] The same kind of logic applies when you think that because you know plenty of "TV babies" who turned out fine, yourself included, it means that the mass media have no pernicious effects. This is a convenient way to dismiss the entire subject, to be sure. But for those interested in measuring the impact of the digital age, as I am, the problem is not so simple.

Rather than looking for simple causes that yield obvious effects, we face the problem of identifying the cumulative effects of a myriad of forces within a constantly changing cultural landscape. Most of the psychological and social effects of concern in this book unfold only gradually and thus have to be measured over time. Historical analysis and longitudinal studies are among the methods used for taking such measures, and these methods are well represented in this book. Also, as emphasized in Grossman's AIDS analogy, we cannot forget that what often appear as strong and immediate causes are only precipitating factors that would have little or no efficacy if it were not for a considerable amount of exposure to other, background factors. Just as violent video games can lower your threshold for acting out violence, chronic exposure to simulated drama, action, and adventure can lower your threshold for boredom and depression. Similarly, chronic exposure to hyperidealized body images can raise the threshold for finding satisfaction in your appearance (or the appearance of a spouse or partner).

As for children in particular, we know from decades of developmental research that the effects of any electronic medium, whether positive or negative, interact in complex ways within the larger context of human development. After all, we should not forget that even very obvious risks for a child, such as divorce, sexual abuse, an alcoholic parent, or adoption, do not necessarily have a single and thus predictable effect. The effects I will go on to describe are profound, but this still does not imply exactly the same effect for everyone. In fact, such a simplistic view of how we are affected by our environment is itself a reflection of our failure to recognize the growing complexity of reality and truth in the world around us.

PART II

THE LONG JOURNEY INTO DIGITOPIA

[W]hen a new technology is introduced into a culture, that culture is forever and permanently changed, through and through. The change is not additive, but ecological. It permeates, like a thimbleful of red dye dropped into a barrel of water. Every molecule of that barrel of water is transformed. . . . Similarly, if you drop the Internet (or the telephone, or TV) into an existing culture, you don't end up with the Internet plus that old culture: you end up with an utterly new culture. The new hyperculture saturates every molecule of our brains—although so gradually, and so subtly, that we have no way to perceive that it's happening. All we see are the observable effects—on ourselves and on each other.

Kalle Lasn and Bruce Grierson, Adbusters

A SHORT HISTORY

OF THE DIGITAL SELF

first stripped naked, then jacked in,

and soon to be downloaded

In an earlier essay on "the one and only reality," I suggested the paradox of your not really knowing what reality is. To start off this next set of essays, I will suggest another seeming paradox, namely that you do not really know who you are.

By this I mean that most of us have little or no grasp of who we are as compared to earlier people in earlier times. Most people take the view that, yes, they live very different lives from people of previous generations, but few realize the considerable extent to which the emerging digital mind of today differs from, say, the American mind of three centuries ago. Certainly, there are radical differences among individuals living within the same moment in history; however, there are also radical differences in the life of the mind that correspond with changes that have taken place in the technology of everyday life.

As with Marshall McLuhan's analysis of the "sensory mandate" of television in 1964, sometimes the transformative effects of media have been anticipated.[1] Another example is Oliver Wendell Holmes, who immediately saw the power of photography to, as he suggested in 1859, engage in a totalizing conquest over matter. With form "divorced" from matter, Holmes noted, "We have got the fruit of creation now, and need not trouble ourselves with the core. Every conceivable object of Nature and Art will soon scale off its surface for us. Men will hunt all curious, beautiful, grand objects, as they hunt the cattle in South America, for their skins, and leave the carcasses as of little worth."[2] As we shall see, Holmes's insights turned out to be especially prophetic with regard to motion pictures, which did not appear until several decades later. Still another example applies to an even earlier time, when, with the appearance of the alphabet and writing, numerous cultures regulated the use of texts, believing as they did that abstract signs with the power of meaning were too potent to be handled by just anyone.[3] Here we also find Plato, who in 374 B.C. asked, "And shall we just carelessly allow children to hear . . . tales which may be devised by casual persons, and to receive into their minds ideas for the most part the very opposite of those which we should want them to have when they are grown up?"[4] Plato's writings are regularly covered in university courses, but imagine what he would say if he were writing today.

Before looking at the impact of media technology more closely, let me clarify briefly what I mean by media technology. *Media* is, of course, the plural form of the word *medium,* which refers to anything that acts as an intermediate, or intervening substance. This simple clarification can take us far, for it directs us to the idea of something that affects or mediates the relationship between two entities. In the case of human beings, media technologies come between us and the physical and social world, which is why technologies involving language, writing, printing, projecting, and computing can be grouped together.[5] On the other hand, while it's true that these are all media technologies, they are also very different from one another. Each represents a quantum leap forward in the degree to which it pushed people's lives away from concrete reality and into abstraction. The eventual outcome would be, as was suggested by the historian Daniel Boorstin, a "thicket of unreality which stands between us and the facts of life."[6]

The overall story of how this came about—of how the digital age came into being and what its origins tell us about where we might be headed in the digital near future—is a story of past, present, and future selves, with humanity first stripped naked, then jacked in, and finally downloaded into a virtual machine. Let's look at these chronologically.

Stripped naked: As indigenous stories from the honored past were replaced by commercial stories of a romanticized future, life in the modern world began to lose its depth and richness of meaning. In the oral tradition, the mind was carried into the past in order to educate the young about the established ways of their world. Stories helped cultivate a mental realm that was more or less in harmony with the facticity of everyday reality. By contrast, the more popular stories on offer today carry people into a make-believe world as a form of abandonment of the here and now. In short, the truth that served as a guide to the present was substituted by a lie that serves as an escape from it. This reversal of fortunes did not have profound implications until the electronic age, however, when virtual worlds leaped from the printed word on the page to the three-dimensional image on the screen. At this moment, the two key ingredients for a digital tomorrow fell into place: America's unquenchable desire for something always newer or better and the progressive evolution of plugged-in technologies that could, like an addictive drug, momentarily satisfy it.

Jacked in: In the postmodern world, virtual reality offers refuge for the naked self, reinforcing people's flight from everyday reality and encouraging a further abandonment of the here and now. The fact that we have become increasingly jacked in is both a consequence of and a reason for the failing state of the American mind. All this began as the medium of the message shifted from the low-definition realm of the spoken word to what we have now: the ever-advancing realm of virtualization. High-definition media require little imagination and effort and present an increasingly realistic experience. This consists of everything from music (the CD) to television (DTV) to video (DVD) to film (digital special effects, digital sound and projection) to social interactions (digital simulcast, mobile phones, Webcams, videoconferencing). As contrasted with unmediated human engagement in the world, from dancing to competing to drawing to gardening to writing to cooking to engaging in face-to-face discourse or intercourse, these media, like those that came before them, are just that: technologies that mediate rather than facilitate meaningful human connections. As one writer put it, *"Unmediated* is a great word: It means 'without media,' without the in-between layer that makes direct experience almost impossible. Media interferes with our capacity to experience naturally, spontaneously, and genuinely, and thereby spoils our capacity for some important kinds of personal 'truths.' "[7] Stanley Crouch gave the following example of this when asked the question of whether digital technology can enhance, or make more true, the music we hear recorded:

> Presence—that's the one thing you can't record. No one who's ever been at a performance that's been recorded has ever heard anything vaguely like what they heard when it was being played. . . . I was at the famous Charles Mingus concert in Monterey in 1964 that was recorded. What I heard played and on the recording are two completely different things. See, you can't record the presence of Mingus and his band, and the feeling in the air outside, and all that. That's all part of the sound too. No machinery can do that. OK, you can make a better recording of something played than you could in, say, 1925. But . . . the purely human thing, of the experience, that can't be recorded.[8]

The result of this trend toward the simulation of everyday life is, as we saw in Part I, the blurring of the boundaries between what should and should not be counted as "real." And as the postmodern mind becomes even more confused about what counts as real, a mismatch arises between where your expectations and desires are cultivated and the only place where they could be (but are not) realized. Until you live in a total virtual culture, you will always have to realize (or try to realize) your wants and needs in the unplugged world. Yet as these needs and wants are conditioned by simulated possibilities in the plugged-in world, the real world becomes increasingly incapable of satisfying them. The result of this double shift is that the virtual worlds on offer in contemporary society now serve less to enhance your real life than to substitute it with artificial ones.

This creates myriad problems for the self. Consider the husband who abandons his real relationship with his wife for virtual relationships in cyberspace. Or consider the child who has abandoned the outside world of active social play for the indoor pseudodrama of video games, which are essentially passive. These examples illustrate the abandonment of the unplugged world for plugged-in virtual realities. Consider the digitally enhanced films (*Titanic, The Perfect Storm, The Matrix*) constructed at a cost of hundreds of millions of dollars. Or consider the anorexic "pleasure model" that is digitally perfected and presented as reality—and then displayed to all girls and women as they pass through the gauntlet of the supermarket checkout line. These examples illustrate the quest for a hyperreality that can never be reproduced in the material world. Consider the channel surfer who never stops surfing long enough to watch more than a few moments of any single television program (or a Web surfer who browses aimlessly for hours on end). Or consider the frustration growing numbers of people are experiencing under conditions of slowness, including computer and road rage. Computer rage illustrates how the quality of people's experience has been forfeited for a mere quantity of it; road rage illustrates how living in a digitally programmed world creates an even greater need for constant speed. Last, consider the collapse of geographic distance by e-mail and the freedom of being able to check one's e-mail at any time or in any place. Or consider the rise of online shopping and the prospect of a virtual downtown. These examples illustrate how life in the digital village of tomorrow comes at the price of losing the whole neighborhood today.

Downloaded: As virtual reality wires the mind for a digital tomorrow, the possibility of inhabiting an all-encompassing digital matrix is appearing on the horizon, creating the specter of total assimilation with digital machines roaming the earth. As Howard Reingold summarized it, "Print and radio tell; stage and film show; cyberspace embodies."[9] Seeing this future possibility requires that we follow the trajectory of the digital age out into the not-so-distant future, looking at the very latest developments in computer architecture, robotics, artificial intelligence, nanotechnology, and cybernetics (more on this in Part IV). This raises the very real possibility that technology will one day help people to live a total cybernetic existence, either of their own choosing or dictated by the rational imperatives of sentient machines that have seized control of the world. Although such talk may sound a bit premature, as not all these technological pursuits will succeed, I think most people would be surprised to know that scientists and philosophers are already attempting to estimate the probability that humans will become extinct. This might occur because of a biotechnological disaster, because terrorists or a rogue nation release self-replicating machines into the air or water to eliminate a particular species or race, or because machines determine humans to be what they most certainly are: expendable.

—

There you have it, a short, short history of the digital self: stripped naked, jacked in, and downloaded. It sounds like science fiction, I admit. Even so, this does not mean these potentialities are all far off in the distant future. As we shall see presently, each revolutionary step in media technology has taken place after only a fraction of the time taken for the previous revolution. The last of them—from analog to digital—took only about thirty-five years.

UNPLUGGED MEDIA

indigenous oral cultures and the first four selves

Although you stand at the dawn of a new digital age, you are not standing entirely at the beginning of a new era. For us humans, it has been a long journey into digitopia, and we are not there yet. When we are, the birth of human culture that began with the word will end in a digital nanosecond, when the last little bit of brain biochemistry is digitally coded and then transmitted into a virtual machine.

What I want to show in this and the following two essays, albeit only in the most summary way, is that we can identify at least six distinct phases of selfhood that correspond with critical moments of technological change. My goal is to reveal the extent to which people's embedding within the social and ecological realities of the past has been destroyed, with other, constructed realities layered over them, one on top of the next. You can then begin to see just how mediated your experience of reality is, with your life falling further into a matrix of simulated possibilities, where rules and constraints are less natural or ecological and more technological.

These six selves include the preverbal self, the oral self, the literal self, the historical self, the visual self, and finally the digital self.

Corresponding to each shift in selfhood is a revolutionary shift in media technology. For example, the primitive, nonverbal self—if we can even call it a "self"—transmuted into a radically different, oral self many thousands of years ago as spoken languages gradually developed. Building on the development of complex spoken languages, each pushing a new self into being, have been the subsequent technologies of writing, printing, projecting, and computing. Note, however, that each of these new technologies has complicated rather than replaced those that came before. Instead of replacing books, for example, television and computers altered the mental environment in which they are now forced to survive (hence the e-book).[1]

When we compare the technology of preverbal *Homo sapiens* with technology today, it immediately becomes clear that technology destroys as it creates. I'm not referring to the ecological destruction of the planet, although that's significant as well; what I'm referring to is the destruction of certain ways of being, certain ways of knowing, and certain relationships humans once had with their immediate surroundings. That is to say, media technology naturally frames experience and shores up meaning in such a way that it cannot but structure or restructure the habits of the mind and the layout of the world. It is for this reason that Marshall McLuhan said that media technologies become an extension of ourselves.

When people lose an arm or leg in life they often experience what is called a phantom limb. That is, they continue to experience the sensation, weight, and perhaps the ache of the limb despite its absence. This is because somatic experience is represented not in the limb but in the neural circuits of your brain. Media as extensions of ourselves are no different. The technologies that mediate your experience, like the limbs that mediate your physical interaction with your surroundings, acquire a level of neural internalization that makes them a natural extension of yourself. The technologies of communication, of entertainment, of education, of work, of medicine become part and parcel of what constitutes your reality. They transform your relationship with the world, and without them you are likely to feel incomplete. This helps explain why you overlook just how virtual your life has become, experiencing each successive layer of mediated and abstracted reality as perfectly natural and real.

When considering how media technologies have transformed us, one thinks of the savage mind and the undomesticated thought of tribal man. But it is not far from the truth to suggest that early humans had something that a marginal but growing number of people desperately want today: an intense, intimate relationship with their immediate physical surroundings. One thinks here of the growing popularity of "adventure" and "experiential" travel and mountain climbing, including of mountains as daunting as Mount Everest. In fact, I wonder how many people would sign up today for a real-life (and death) version of *Survivor* (although one also thinks of the millions more who would much prefer living these adventures vicariously through books such as *Into Thin Air,* movies such as *The Perfect Storm,* and shows such as *Survivor*). Claude Lévi-Strauss knew this well: "When we make the mistake of thinking that the Savage is governed only by organic and economic needs, we forget that he levels the same reproach at us, and that to him his own desire for knowledge seems more balanced than ours."[2]

As the preverbal (or first) self evolved into the oral self, subsequent to the development of complex oral languages, a price had to be paid. As we shall see, however, this price of cultural evolution came only gradually, as oral communication evolved into a codified system of language, with the alphabetization of the popular mind.

The oral self existed roughly fifty thousand years before the development of writing, although primary oral cultures still exist today. As language and culture developed over this vast period, people began to live in larger social groups, and the mind gradually became animated by something other than direct, pure experience.

As the first and most powerful form of information technology ever to appear, language obviously served communication functions that were much more efficient and effective than simple gestures or grunts. But this is not the aspect of language that eventually transformed the life of the mind. As language is acquired, it creates a scaffolding on which people's thoughts are thereafter constructed.

"I have forgotten the word I intended to say, and my thought unembodied, returns to the realm of shadows."[3] This bit of poetry nicely sums up the point that even in early oral cultures, language had the effect of animating thoughts and imagination through words, concepts, expressions, and metaphors. As it did, it also gained the capacity to convey information about events that went beyond the present moment. That is to say, language allowed the cultivation of stories. It created folklore and myth.

In doing so, language also acquired the capacity to do something else—something that would make it and all subsequent media technologies very alluring; namely, the capacity to transport the mind to another time and place. As noted, while stories today have the primary escapist function of removing us from the present, language in primary oral cultures did not have this effect. To the contrary, in the oral tradition of spoken rather than written words, language was organic to people's lives. It was used, as folklorist Jack Zipes notes, "to create communal bonds in the face of inexplicable forces of nature."[4] That is, it served to clothe the naked self. It was also used to carry the imagination into the past in order to educate younger individuals about the established ways of their world. Accordingly, stories helped cultivate the mind in ways that promoted social harmony, while also educating individuals about the facts, or facticity, of everyday life.

David Abram, in *The Spell of the Sensuous,* provides a description of the role of language in the "indigenous oral cultures" of Native Americans. As an account of contemporary oral cultures, his examples have the positive feature of existing side by side with our own, highly abstracted culture. On Apache society, he writes:

> The moral efficacy of the landscape—this power of the land to ensure mindful and respectful behavior in the community—is mediated by a whole class of stories that are regularly recounted within the village. These narratives tell of persons who underwent misfortune as a consequence of violating Apache standards for right behavior; they tell of individuals who, as a result of act-

ing impulsively or in open defiance of Apache custom, suffered humiliation, illness, or death.[5]

The emergence of language set the stage, however, for a series of other developments in media technology. These technologies led to levels of abstraction that no longer had the effect of bringing people into closer contact with their natural surroundings or one another. This brings us to the third self, the *literal self,* which would be in existence roughly four thousand years before the next shift in selfhood, to the historical self, which came with the advent of the printing press.

The impact of language as an information technology would not be limited to oral stories. The influential analyses of twentieth-century minds such as Vygotsky and Wittgenstein have forced us to accept that language has not just a descriptive capacity, but also a prescriptive one.[6] What this means is that learning a language not only allows you to communicate—"Pass the pepper, please"—it also shapes the way the mind thinks. "More than any other single invention," writes Walter Ong in *Orality and Literacy,* "writing has transformed human consciousness. . . . Without writing, the literate mind would not and could not think as it does, not only when engaged in writing, but normally even when it is composing its thoughts in oral form."[7]

As oral cultures evolved into literate cultures and the oral mind into the literal mind, the capacity of language to act as a lens that filters and colors people's sense of the world was increased. It also had the effect, as suggested by Ong, of privatizing the mind—of turning the mind from its outward focus on others and one's surroundings to an inward focus on oneself (interior monologue). In primary oral cultures, the use of language was almost exclusively a shared, public activity between speakers and listeners. With writing and then with printing, however, this all changed, and language became a source not of attraction but of abstraction.

As the oral self evolved culturally into the literal self, the transportive capacity of language also shot forward, such that thoughts, first captured in sound, were now captured as permanent signs. The result was that stories could be put down on tablets, scrolls, manuscripts, and texts, which meant a further abstraction of experience. The reason for this is simple: when stories became portable, they could be removed from their place of origin and be read (or, as was more likely the case, listened to) elsewhere. By infiltrating local villages or cultures, stories could produce a similar effect; that is, they could remove people (in mind if not in body) from their place of origin. Such a state of affairs appeared in Europe as early as 1000 B.C., although it would not be until the Middle Ages that this began to take place on a significant scale.

As this suggests, writing did not instantly mean printing or widespread literacy. The former came much later, in the fifteenth century, when printing technology was developed in Europe by Johannes Gutenberg (the Gutenberg press is dated at 1448; the Chinese had developed similar movable-type technology by 1040). As Philip Marchand notes about the Gutenberg press, "Everything about this invention . . . was a tremendous victory for the abstract, the mechanistic, the visual."[8] Thus we encounter a new phase of selfhood, the *historical self,* as *historia* begins gradually to replace—or join with?—*mythos.*

As with earlier transformations of selfhood in the West, the emergence of a fully historical self was a long time coming. Monks of the Middle Ages, for example, did not read their manuscripts as you read books today, but rather read them aloud quietly to themselves while attempting to memorize every word.[9] Still, over time, printing presses led to the mass availability of texts, which led in turn to growing literacy. By 1500, roughly 40,000 editions and a total of 2 million copies of books had been printed; with presses appearing across Europe, 200 million copies would be published in the sixteenth century.[10] "If the phonetic alphabet fell like a bombshell on tribal man, the printing press hit him like a 100-megaton H-bomb," wrote Marshall McLuhan.[11] Books and literacy brought the historical self into being, and with it the modern age. Indeed, nearly everything modern about modernity could not have come about without the development of the printing press—its science, its literature, its social progress in human rights, its music, its art, its fashion.

As an example, consider Betty Friedan's *The Feminine Mystique*. Here is a book that created an alternative world into which women could enter to find a better reality. Not only did it provide women with another way of knowing, it also had a huge positive impact on the lives of many women. By comparison, consider another product of modernity: daytime television. What is the relationship between *The Feminine Mystique* and *Days of Our Lives*? The answer is obvious: one shows women a way out of a disastrous world of illusions, and one locks them right back in. And we should not forget how many readers of *The Feminine Mystique* have gone on to be avid watchers of daytime dramas. These are the media technologies that allowed modernity to be made.

Obviously it would be a mistake to conclude that the loss of oral cultures was an unmitigated disaster, even if it did tear us from the social and ecological habitats in which we had evolved. With writing and then printing, the historical self ushered in an age of enlightenment, and for the modern self there could never be a going back to an oral mind or an oral culture. But the inevitability of it all does not negate the fact that something about the human self was lost in the translation, much as something crucial would be lost in the digital translation of social interactions through cyberspace. Life was becoming more complex, the mind was becoming more confused, and the future was becoming a burden for Western societies, focused as they had become on continual technological, industrial, and economic change. Ong sums it up well in *Orality and Literacy*, writing:

> Oral cultures indeed produce powerful and beautiful verbal performances of high artistic and human worth, which are no longer even possible once writing has taken possession of the psyche. Nevertheless, without writing, human consciousness cannot achieve its fuller potentials, cannot produce other beautiful and powerful creations. In this sense, orality needs to produce and is

destined to produce writing. . . . There is hardly any oral culture or a predominantly oral culture left in the world today that is not somehow aware of the vast complex of powers forever inaccessible without literacy.[12]

This is a vast complex of powers indeed. It would not be long before the world created through books and literacy would overwhelm the historical self, pushing a new, *visual* self into being. This came about through a series of rapid technological changes, all of which were part of a new age of technology: the electric age of illuminated media.

PLUGGED-IN MEDIA

child of projection: the fifth self

The preverbal self, the oral self, the literal self, and the historical self: these are the first phases of selfhood to develop as part of our cultural evolution, each with a distinct physical and mental environment in which the self appeared, lived, and worked.

The fifth self, the *visual self,* which came into being in the electronic age, did so early in the twentieth century with the arrival of silent motion pictures. As was suggested earlier, and as should be clear by now, each successive transformation in media technology has unfolded in only a portion of the time it took for the previous one. Combined with the fact that each transformation also brought with it a vast increase in the amount of information carried by the latest technology, it should also be clear that the rate at which concrete reality is being reduced to abstraction is a highly exponential one.[1] As Jacques Ellul describes it in *The Technological Society,* the individual has "been liberated little by little from physical constraints, but he is all the more the slave of abstract ones. He acts through intermediaries and consequently has lost contact with reality."[2] Projected out into the digital future, the accelerated pace of technological evolution means that what seems like an impossibility today—the digitization and downloading of all mind and matter into a virtual machine—could very much be a reality of tomorrow.

With regard to film and the fifth self, let me stress that if people could lose themselves in books—as they did with even greater zeal after the development of the pocket paperback in 1939—this was only the beginning of what would eventually take place as the message of the medium was plugged in. While film has many features that set it apart from text, both perceptual and cultural, it must be remembered that film and texts do share one feature: as media, both are predominantly visual.

Viewed in this way, we can see how printing created a bridge between oral cultures of earlier times and the visually dominated culture of today. As noted, oral culture relied on human-generated sound to make meaning; it took place in acoustic space. As language took the form of the visual sign, however, it was severed from its inherent ties to the community, and thus the meaning provided through language was no longer necessarily social. When language entered into photographic space, the printed word was in trouble, as there was no chance of its competing against the flickering images that language had inspired. It is common today to find people lamenting the abandonment of the book for more indulgent visual technologies such as film and television. What is not so common, however, is finding anyone who realizes that this abandonment had been written all along, in the fine print.

As it turns out, a whole host of accomplished writers have covered this ground, their books challenging the triumph of media technology over human affairs and human reason. Among many others, these include Jean Baudrillard's *Simulacra and Simulation* and *The Perfect Crime,* Daniel Boorstin's *The Image,* Stuart Ewen's *All Consuming Images,* Neal Gabler's *Life the Movie,* Marshall McLuhan's *Understanding Media,* Michael Parenti's *Make-Believe Media,* and Neil Postman's *Amusing Ourselves to Death.* I have neither the space to retell, nor the capacity to tell better, what these and other writers have told so well. Consequently, I will simply suggest to interested readers that they pursue these texts for what they find lacking here. That said, let me make a few remarks about how the technology of projection first opened a portal into the world of hyperreality.

For thousands of years media technology had the magical effect of creating meaning independent of direct experience. Stories in oral cultures did this, as did written accounts. Until the emergence of projected visual images (and sounds), however, this meaning came in a low-tech medium that still required the direct involvement of the speaker, the reader, or the listener. By comparison, film was visual candy. First-time viewers of early cinema did not just find it a compelling *lifelike* experience, they found it a compelling *real-life* experience. Being awestruck is one thing; leaping out of one's chair at the sight of an oncoming train is quite another.[3] What this means is that film did not just tell dramatic stories, it aspired to replace them with a hyperreality that concealed their nature as just stories.[4]

Entering a cinema for the first time, one steps across the line into passive virtuality. For projected media have as a principal goal not just the reproduction of real human experiences, as both good and bad books can do this, but the reproduction of the same sensory effects produced by direct experience. As everyone knows, movies were made out of bits of photographed reality, although these bits were usually assembled in ways that produced not a mimicking of reality but a more exciting, more dramatic, more romantic, more comical, more idealistic, more uplifting version of it—in short, a hyperreality. In *All Consuming Images,* Stuart Ewen described this photographic reconstituting of reality as creating "a vast mobile market in images [where] . . . the *look* of the visible world could now be easily, and inexpensively reproduced."[5]

The power of such a technological dreamscape was great on its own. But it was made even greater by what was taking place simultaneously in the unplugged realm. With urbanization, factory life, and the expanding industrial society, the mind of the worker was transformed on two sides. Susan Buck-Morris makes the point well in her recent book *Dreamworld and Catastrophe,* suggesting that there was a radical change in the relationship between mind and material reality—a change that would enhance the attraction of the new visual technology:

> Under conditions of modern technology, the aesthetic system undergoes a dialectical reversal. The human sensorium changes from a mode of being "in touch" with reality into a means of blocking out of reality. Aesthetics—sensory perception—becomes *an*aesthetics, a numbing of the senses' cognitive capacity that destroys the human organism's power to respond politically even when self-preservation is at stake. Someone who is "past experiencing," writes [Walter] Benjamin, is "no longer capable of telling . . . proven friend . . . from mortal enemy."[6]

To date, the most explicit form of the desire to fully simulate reality, still in its early stages, has been virtual reality (VR) technology.[7] This consists of the wrapping of media equipment around the senses to simulate ongoing experiences; as a person acts and reacts, these outputs are fed into a computer, which then stimulates the senses, including the visual sense, to create the appropriate experience. What could conceivably come after VR technology is at this point science fiction. For example, there is the "jacking in" described in cyberpunk science fiction novels such as William Gibson's classic *Neuromancer* or Marge Piercy's *He, She, and It*. There is also the related example of "downloading" of the mind into a virtual machine, as shown in movies such as *The Matrix*. All these examples are extensions of the basic fact that projected media technologies are designed to re-create reality, which is of course why television has been transformed over the years from black-and-white to color to big screens and wide screens to digital TV programming and hardware. The latest along these lines is the Elumens VisionStation, which offers a personal IMAX-like experience via a two-by-five-foot concave screen, all at the price of only $19,995.

In the context of this reconstituting of reality, the visual self became the first self to face, however unknowingly, the choice between spending time in a primary versus a secondary reality. When film first appeared in theaters, this was at best a limited opportunity. With the introduction of the small screen, however, the opportunity became a continuous one (at least for the normal waking hours). (Note that the speed with which television situated itself in the American household was far faster than for any other media technology, including radio and telephone; in the 1950s, the number of homes with TV sets went from 10 to 90 percent, and the arrival of the box has since been correlated with a massive decrease in social participation in civic life.)[8] The visual self was, in other words, the first self to experience the "replacement of a reliable world of durable objects by a world of flickering images that make it harder to distinguish reality from fantasy."[9]

This brings us to a crucial moment in how media technology came to be used to condition in us a lust for impossibilities. This might be described as a kind of double double whammy. The first double whammy is the current state of media technology: first is its long-standing capacity to construct meaning independent of direct experience, second is its better-developed capacity to project this decontextualized meaning in a highly realistic form. Coupled together, these capacities of media technology would be used to condition the mind with ideas, images, and moods that looked and felt as though they were real but were not.

The second double whammy dovetails with the first and deals with the question of why the realm of simulated reality has been a compelling one for both the arbiters of reality and the consumers of it: first there is the fact that, for hundreds of years, children of modern societies have been growing up in a progressively more abstract world, with each generation more or less oblivious to the changes in the nature of experience that took place in previous generations; second is the fact that millions of people, especially in the United States, have been experiencing a decline in the integrity of social reality and, along with it, the rise of the commodity solution. (By the commodity solution I mean that an expanding corporate world has emerged to exploit the growing culture of discontent.) Coupled together, these forces have determined both the content and the power of mass media, popular culture, and lifestyle capitalism.

Taken in full, this double double whammy has meant the emergence of a mass marketing of ideas and images with two primary functions: the manufacturing of desire and the selling of simulated experiences that seek either to satisfy it (in some fleeting sense) or to provide a distraction from it. It is in the context of this new consumer culture that we turn next to the rise of the sixth self: the *digital self.*

THE COMING OF DIGITAL AGE

cyberpunks and the sixth self

In the age of digital computers, the digital self appears—finally! Unfortunately, if you are beyond your adolescent years, chronologically speaking, you are probably not a candidate for full membership in the order of digital selfhood—not even if you're reading this book on a handheld computer. What is more likely the case is that you yourself are, or are becoming, some kind of visual-digital hybrid. To see why, we must look at how the digital self differs from the visual self.

The digital self is different in two fundamental ways: one quantitative, the other qualitative. First, relative to the visual self, people born into the digital age, especially those who grow up with cyberspace closer than the house next door, have a vast amount of exposure to the rhythms and images that come with the digitization of entertainment, telecommunications, education, and work. This simply means that the digital self is "better" adapted to (and more dependent upon) the present technological society than is the visual self. This should be clear to anyone who has spent time with the "cyberpunks" of the digital age: their minds have evolved alongside digitization and cyberspace, and thus they are very much in sync with it. A lead story in *Content* magazine: "They're brilliant, ambitious, and almost intuitively gifted at technology. A new generation of whiz kids are gaining unprecedented power and authority—and, as a new study shows, they're reshaping the American family."[1] An article in *The New York Times:* "Choosing a Salary or Tuition: Some Young Computer Experts Say No to College."[2] An essay in *Context* magazine: "The hyper-wired customers you'll encounter tomorrow have already arrived. They are on college campuses today. . . . [College students] are natives in cyberspace while their elders are immigrants."[3] These are the digital recruits of a new, "cyberpunk" generation.

Turning to the second difference, it can also be said that individuals born into the digital information age will acquire a different worldview than did the visual self born before it. This idea of a qualitatively different worldview is premised on the assumption that your most basic sense of the world becomes more or less fixed during your formative years. Yes, education can open your eyes to the world around you, but there is, I think, a deeper level of understanding that is not so easily changed.

Researchers have recently shown, for instance, that not just the content of thought but the very habits of thought can vary among individuals, and in fact they do so in the case of people who have grown up in different cultures (for example, in Japan as opposed to in the United States). Experimental research is now confirming that people of Eastern cultures think more holistically—that is, they pay more attention to context and incorporate personal experience to a greater degree—while Westerners are more apt to be analytical and abstract in their thinking, deemphasizing context and personal experience.[4] We know these are not racial/biological differences, moreover, because they are correlated with cultural experience and not necessarily with race. There is also research showing that these cognitive patterns are not easily erased by later experience. Looking at what is called "frame switching," researchers have shown that individuals growing up in a multicultural context—for instance, a child who lives in the United States but is raised within a traditional Chinese family—

adapt to this cultural mix by switching back and forth between different cultural lenses.[5] The fact that multiple cultural frames remain intact while one adapts to a new culture, rather than undergoing fusion, suggests that early ways of understanding the world are indeed resistant to change.

If the worldview of the digital self does differ from that of the visual self and will continue to differ to an even greater degree in the near future, as research suggests, what is the nature of this difference? In the most general sense, this difference is an existential one. Children of cyberculture have a different sense of the world and the future that lies ahead. They are growing up in a reality that is highly fluid, from the social relationships that they observe around them to the technological changes taking place in their immediate physical environment at home and at school to the breakdown in the barriers between the material and digital world. They are also growing up in a world saturated with commerce, where the three F's—fashion, fame, and fortune—rule over the three R's—reading, writing, and 'rithmetic. The results are obviously very variable, but the general effect is that life is lived on the surface of a thinly coated, friction-free reality.[6] Nothing is felt deeply, nothing is of any great importance, all is transient, all is relative, and image is more important than any substantive reality.

There is also a geographic difference between the visual and the digital self. This concerns changes taking place in the dimensions of time and space. Born into an oral culture, the self acquired a cyclical sense of time and a highly circumscribed sense of geographic space; born into a print culture, the historical self acquired a sense of linear time and a global sense of space; finally, born into a digital age, the digital self acquires a sense of timeless time and placeless space. In the most elementary sense, this means that children of cyberculture are connected to a twenty-four-hour culture that never sleeps. It also means they have significantly weaker ties to the idea of inhabiting a particular physical place called "home." In cyberjargon, home is not where you hang your hat but where you post your chat name. What the social and psychological implications of these changes will be is at this point far from clear. On the one hand, it would seem that the digital self would be better adapted to, and thus better prepared for, the digital world that is now emerging. On the other hand, it's not at all clear that the structure of the digital mind will be a stable one. Of course, this begs a larger question: Under what cultural conditions does the human mind flourish, and under what conditions does it crash? This question will be explored in some detail in Part IV, on the geography of digitopia.

Whatever the future holds for the fully developed digital self, we can trust it will be different from the reality faced by us virtual-digital hybrids today, caught as we are between the illusions of virtuality and the disillusions of the unplugged world. We can also trust it to be different from the seventh self—the *cybernetic self.* In fact, as with the first self—the preverbal self—there is a question as to whether this terminal self should even be considered a legitimate self. If selfhood is a concept used to describe human beings as they emerge out of the contingencies of the cultural realm, perhaps the "cybernetic self" will be not really a self at all, but rather a whole new kind of being. Might not the self that emerges in history also disappear back into it?

PART III

THE PSYCHOLOGY OF THE DIGITAL AGE

Our machines are disturbingly lively, and we ourselves are frighteningly inert.

Donna Haraway

A DIGITAL ETHOS

Just log on, jack in, and drop out

Not long before I began conceptualizing this book, I was in Britain lecturing on hyperculture and its impact on the developing minds of young children. One evening in London I entered an Internet café for, I must admit, the first time. It was relatively late, and I was hoping to locate a phone number I had tucked away somewhere out in cyberspace. As I walked in I saw a smattering of heads. All the clientele was computer-interfaced, eyes transfixed on glowing screens, right hands riding the backs of mice. Like William Gibson, who came up with the idea of cyberspace after noting how mesmerized individuals were when playing video games in amusement arcades, I was struck by the degree to which people were themselves logged on and jacked in. Not a single social interaction was to be heard or seen. I'm sure people were chatting away with strangers from all corners of the globe, but I wondered how long I would have to wait for Malcolm de Chazal's insight—"Only the human face can milk our glance dry"—to come true. Is the human connection being replaced by the technological connection? Is simple human interaction not good enough anymore?

After my brief stay in London I continued to wonder about how we are becoming digitally mastered. If media become an extension of ourselves, as Marshall McLuhan noticed almost four decades ago, what will we as a society become in the digital age? Perhaps it's the digital matrix itself that we are becoming, which would explain why the digital matrix is, like the eyes through which we view it, so utterly transparent. As the film *The Matrix* reminds us, one cannot escape from that of which one is not aware, and thus there seems to be a real risk in ignoring just how far we have traveled into this electronic otherworld and how much further into it digitization will take us. Jean Baudrillard warns, "There will be no end to this frenzied race around the Möbius strip where the surface of meaning perpetually feeds into the surface of illusions, unless the illusion of meaning were to win out once and for all, which would put an end to the world."[1]

Meanwhile, in the prevailing absence of awareness that a journey into digitopia is under way, a prominent ethos of the twenty-first century is becoming crystal—or is it now digitally?—clear: Log on, jack in, and drop out.

Here we have Timothy Leary's psychedelic vision of the 1960s— "Turn on, tune in, and drop out"—adapted to the digital age. Notice, however, that this reformulation of the Leary mantra has a decidedly different flavor. Leary urged a generation to drop out of institutional consciousness and tune in to one another. People were to give up worshiping the false gods of the war and culture industries and return to a simpler, communal life.[2] By contrast, when you log on, jack in, and drop out today, you are not dropping out of commercial consciousness. You are clinging to it ever so tightly, dropping out of reality instead.

Welcome to hyperculture, where progress seems to move ever so quickly, but seemingly in reverse. Now the motion is toward the technological and away from the social, toward the complex and away from the simple, toward work and away from leisure, toward the unreal and away from the real, toward the synthetic and away from the sensuous. Why? As we shall see in this third section, there is some method to this madness. What we shall see specifically is that this question forces a consideration of the psychology of the digital age. We shall also see how this psychology has developed out of, and reinforces, certain societal structures rooted in consumer capitalism and the ethos of "better living through technology" that it endlessly promotes.

Let us begin by locating ourselves in the present moment, at the dawn of the digital age, in full pursuit of a virtual life.

Each of us likes to believe that we are more or less unencumbered by family, by circumstance, and by history. And to some extent we are. We also like to believe that digital technology lets us do things we could never do before—whether it's never to miss another call, to watch a DVD film while waiting for our plane to arrive, or to orient ourselves on a digital map while driving in a foreign city. Our individualistic, competitive, hurried, and harried society may be exhausting, but it does seem to be creating a variety of new and interesting opportunities.

Yet when we step back and look at the human drama unfolding today, it appears very much as though we are living out our lives on a moving train, one that is headed full speed into the digital unknown. Life on the train seems relatively quiet and calm. But this is merely an illusion created by the fact that the train has almost no windows. If there were more—and this book is a small attempt to let a little more light in—you would realize that your sense of speed, of change, of motion, is very much a restricted one. Historically, as we have seen, the rate at which earthly reality is fusing with the synthetic, the mechanical, and the virtual is picking up speed with incredible force; the train is, in other words, accelerating. Stay on the same tracks long enough, and you are sure to end up in a very different place.

Within the context of everyday life, however, everything seems to be moving with little or no speed; while there are the occasional shakes and vibrations on this train, there is no hint or warning of any dangerous curves to come. Some people are even turning their backs on adding technological complexity to their lives, instead simplifying their lives; that is, they are moving toward the rear of the train. The vast majority are more or less going with the flow; that is, they are sitting in the train.

The point, though, should be obvious: it doesn't really matter in *what* direction any particular individual is moving *on* the train. As long as what we do as a collective society does not reduce the mass, the speed, or the acceleration of the train, we are all headed to digitopia together. It is our destination, with the social and ecological world left behind.

In fact, far from slowing it down, we are, as a collective, feeding the fire at an ever-increasing rate. One can hardly be surprised. With the digital ethos of log on, jack in, and drop out becoming the dominant ethos of our time, the race to inner space seems to be the only train running. After all, look at how far we have already come; look at how much further digitization promises to take us; and look at how globalization seems to give us little choice but to go forward as fast as we can.

Much the same holds from the point of view of work. We are, first of all, in the shadow of the cold-war industries, which means that serving the digital information age represents a central, if not *the* central, industry in American society. If you're not in the service or culture industries and you're not in the medical industry, then you're probably in one of the electronic information industries (by which I do not mean to suggest that these three industries are not overlapping or mutually reinforcing, which they are).

Second, I'm not so sure this is such a great place for the train to stop. My own personal sense is that we are in a position not unlike that of the character Cypher in *The Matrix*. If you have seen the film, you already know that Cypher is among a select few striving to take control of the matrix back from the machine intelligence that created it. As a noninhabitant of the digital matrix, Cypher lives in a bleak, subterranean world, always on the run, where the main source of sustenance is a tasteless, disgusting goop. Faced with such an existence, he begins to entertain the possibility of turning against his comrades, to be reinserted back into the virtual machine.

This scenario challenges us with a delightful philosophical problem. Is it better to live as a free and informed but also lonely and deprived individual outside the machine? Or is it better to live in "decadence" within the relatively plush but totally simulated—and machine-controlled—theater of the matrix? Better to rage against the machine or to live peacefully and submissively within it? Clearly the creators of the film want to push us toward the former, enlightened choice (and not necessarily just with regard to the film). "Free your mind," the lead character, Morpheus, tells us. And while I obviously lean in this direction myself, I do not think we should hurry to draw a conclusion. In fact, in this essay I want only to introduce this philosophical problem, leaving the remainder of the book to try to clarify its full meaning. In the meantime, if you've not seen *The Matrix,* consider it a homework assignment.

At the heart of this choice lies the question of whether a simulated reality can act as a vital surrogate for a material, earthly reality. Recall that the matrix provides a reality that at the neurophysiological level is the same as earthly reality (assuming the matrix works according to the same rules as conventional society does). At the physical level of reality, however, the matrix is nothing but a virtuality-creating machine. As such, the choice may seem quite obvious. Still, a question remains: What if the content of the two realities you are choosing between is not equal? For instance, as illustrated in *The Matrix,* there is the possibility that one could face a choice between life in an obviously inferior corporeal world and life in the digital alternative.

In his award-winning 1974 book on moral philosophy, *Anarchy, State, and Utopia,* Robert Nozick presented his readers with this very problem, asking "Should you plug into this machine for life?"[3] In the year 2000, he returned to this question, arguing that "In a virtual world, we'll long for reality even more."[4] But is this really true? Unfortunately, Nozick has remained trapped all these years in a kind of naturalistic romanticism, assuming that life in the corporeal world is inherently better because it's real—it's natural.[5] For example, he argued in 2000 that "we want not only to experience things a certain way—for instance, our children being happy, our colleagues respecting us—we also want the situation to actually be that way. We don't want our whole life to be an illusion or a delusion, or to be merely virtual." Again I ask: Is this really so, especially today? I'm not at all convinced that we are interested in putting "real life" ahead of the virtual life; nor do I believe the evidence supports such a view. Furthermore, if life in the digital matrix produces an identical neurophysiological experience in terms of both your actions and your consequent experiences, this ends up being a meaningless distinction, especially if, as Nozick himself realizes, you have no awareness that you have turned yourself over to a neurally simulated experience.[6]

Nozick does recognize that in the near future people may choose to spend their days and nights embedded in virtuality, but he argues in turn that "the rest of us are likely to find that choice deeply disturbing." Again I question this conclusion. Nozick argues that most people will reject this "experience machine" because they know that the meaning of life cannot be reduced to a philosophy of electronic hedonism. "We refuse to see ourselves as merely buckets to be filled with happy experiences," he writes. This misses the point, however, since pleasure has nothing to do with it. The ethos of log on, jack in, and drop out is not thriving because people are seeking a hedonistic paradise. However positive or entertaining the virtual experience, the ultimate reason why we are in flight from reality is to escape the unpleasantness of our immediate inner and outer lives, which ranges from boredom and restlessness to anxiety and despair. The virtual life is not so much the opium of the masses; it's the anesthesia of the masses.

In the end, what Robert Nozick proposes may be good moral philosophy—a philosophy about how we *ought* to be and what we *ought* to do with our lives—but as he and everyone else knows, "ought" and "is" are two very different matters, especially in the hyperreal world of today.

Let me add one last thing. The point is not only that the digital self might one day be faced with a choice between a fading reality and a shimmering virtuality. Regardless of our ability to obtain the knowledge and construct the technology that will one day make digitopia more than mere metaphor, the fact remains that this is the world in which we are investing. Thus, a failure to succeed in creating a true digital matrix might turn out to be not a blessing but a disaster. For as long as we continue to abandon the social and ecological world with such exuberance, there may soon be no place else for us to go.

THE SAD AND LONELY
WORLD OF CYBERSPACE

what psychological research can (and cannot)
tell us about america online

With so much energy, attention, and creativity being put to the service of the digital information age, the question arises: Why do we as a society assume there are no significant side effects of building and inhabiting a digital world?

With so few formal studies of what is happening to us psychologically and socially in these digital times, it's often assumed that the digital information age is coming up roses, obviating the need for such concern. Some also believe that it's too early in the game—that the adverse symptoms of living a digital life are too weak or vague—to be able to make a reliable diagnosis at this time. There also appears to be a fear that any encroachment on the development of the digital revolution could hinder it and the e-economy it has stimulated. Yet another view is that the changes taking place are so all-determining that we had just better brace ourselves for them and make the best of whatever comes. In a similar vein, it's often thought that perhaps the psychological and social questions raised by the digital revolution are too complex and too all-encompassing for us to comprehend, let alone respond to in an intelligent manner.

These various attitudes, although common, are largely mistaken. The digital revolution has great promise for transforming us and the world, but not without collateral side effects, some of which, should we allow digital technology to determine its own path, could be much more dramatic than we can imagine today. Neither is it the case that our interests are best served by a hands-off approach, an attitude that was often heard with respect to the Microsoft antitrust case. In truth, the general concern here is not significantly different from one that Marshall McLuhan already expressed forty years ago. As reported by one of his biographers, "McLuhan had spoken of his terror at the disaster civilization faced if mankind could not learn to use new media wisely, adding that this required understanding them in order to control their consequences."[1] A few years later, McLuhan declared, "I wish none of these technologies ever happened. . . . They impress me as nothing but a disaster. They are for dissatisfied people. Why is man so unhappy he wants to change his world? I would never attempt an improvement—my personal preference, I suppose, would be preliterate milieus; but I want to study change to gain power over it."[2]

The hands-off approach to technological development historically and today stems from the prevailing view that technology naturally evolves to meet basic human needs, or at least our basic human nature. "Such is human nature," writes Frederick Allen in *American Heritage* magazine, "illustrating the basic truth that our technologies, like our artistic creations, are and always have been nothing more or less than plain expressions of our human nature."[3] There may be a grain of truth in such statements, but ultimately they're wrong. On the one hand, everything from housing to electricity to refrigeration to mechanized tractors would seem consistent with the view that technology serves our nature and our needs. At the same time, however, the opposite seems equally true. As we have seen in the history of media technology, the life of the mind relative to the social and ecological world has undergone a dramatic adaptation since the arrival of language. The preverbal mind is radically different from the mind infused with language (the oral mind), just as the oral mind is radically different from the mind structured through literacy (the literal mind), the literal mind from the analog mind, and the analog mind from the digital mind. All these transformations were brought about by technologies so powerful that they fast-forwarded cultural evolution, with "human nature" struggling to keep up along the way.

If necessity is the mother of all invention, invention is the father of all necessity. And as Jacques Ellul makes clear in *The Technological Society,* "This new necessity is not natural necessity; natural necessity, in fact, no longer exists. It is technique's necessity, which becomes the more constraining the more nature's necessity fades and disappears."[4]

Having said this, I want to make it clear that in no way am I suggesting that a disastrous outcome is inevitable. The impending future may indeed be shot from a long barrel, but one should not therefore conclude that we have lost all capacity to redirect the digital bullet that is coming our way. The problem has more to do with correcting a severe and long-standing mismatch between two different kinds of knowledge: As a society we are very knowledgeable in the ways of technology and science. As curators of our own destiny, however, we are still like the child who plays with matches. As with this child, one hopes that the proper lessons can be learned, preferably without burning down the house.

In anticipation of such an event, with smoke filling the air, one step that might be taken is to create capable and permanent organizations to monitor developments in this area, just as we have organizations that monitor other aspects of human health and welfare. While media and technology studies have been legitimate academic disciplines for some time, a bridge has never been built between them and the public institutions charged with overseeing the public's well-being. This is partly due to the fact that many people view media and technology studies as essentially anti-American, which they do because their scholars and researchers challenge that most sacred of assumptions; namely, that unfettered technological development is our greatest resource for building a better life.

A related step in this direction would be for us as a society, whether at the public or private level, to encourage the deployment of science in measuring the impact of the digital age. Such an approach has the advantage of taking us above the plane of anecdotal evidence, which is unlikely to be heard above the constant hype concerning the personal, social, economic, and even political opportunities that come with living in a fully wired (and wireless) world. It is already said that our lives are richer and more fun, people's connections with others are greater, the economy couldn't be better, and—as suggested by the use of the World Wide Web for political campaigns—democracy is stronger.[5] Is this really so?

Consider the Internet. The conventional wisdom would have us believe that the Internet will bring new harmony to the world while also ensuring vast economic prosperity for all. Nicholas Negroponte, a senior media guru of the Massachusetts Institute of Technology, has been quoted as saying that the children of tomorrow "are not going to know what nationalism is."[6] As if world peace were not enough, the Internet has also been hailed as a savior of Mother Earth, because it will radically reduce energy consumption and people's dependence on paper. It has been lauded as a prime mover for a new era of social equality, where it will tear down longstanding barriers to the knowledge that less fortunate people are said to need (and only need) to flourish. The Internet has even been identified as the great leveler of power, where a nobody of yesterday can produce a webpage and go head-to-head with CNN. As was argued in an issue of *The Economist* on "What the Internet Cannot Do," the idea of the Internet as a panacea for all of society's woes has little hope of being realized. In fact, researchers have yet to demonstrate even that the overall psychological and social consequences of jacking in to the Net are positive ones.

This brings us to the title of this essay, which derives from a *New York Times* article entitled, "Sad, Lonely World Discovered in Cyberspace."[7] The title aptly summarizes the findings of a report that appeared in 1998 in the American Psychological Association's monthly journal, *American Psychologist:* "Internet Paradox: A Social Technology That Reduces Social Involvement and Psychological Well-being?"[8] This $1.5 million study was conducted by researchers at Carnegie Mellon University and is the only longitudinal study of "America online" published to date.

Using longitudinal measures, the Carnegie Mellon researchers were able to track changes in individuals' social behavior and psychological well-being as they gradually positioned themselves in cyberspace. As the study's 169 participants went online for one to two years, the researchers measured changes in their communication with family members, the size of the participants' social circles, and their levels of depression and loneliness. What they found was that each and every measure showed an overall negative trajectory *for these users.* Specifically, the data showed that more time spent online meant less communication with immediate family members, a shrinking of one's social circle, and increases in self-reports of both loneliness and depression (these results have also been replicated in a less rigorous study, which showed similar effects for individuals who spent more than five hours a week online).[9]

Several other findings reinforce the significance of the study. First, these results were common among individuals regardless of how attracted they initially were to going online. In other words, the social and psychological impact of this technology was essentially the same regardless of how lonely or depressed the user was at the outset. These results also occurred despite the fact that most of these individuals used their time online in a social manner—that is, to communicate via e-mail rather than surf the Web. In fact, even those who went online only a few hours per week experienced some decline in their psychological well-being, even if all they did was e-mail. The researchers had assumed that because the Internet is a more interactive and self-determined environment than television, it would not produce the same kind of couch-potato malaise.[10] It nevertheless did for some or most individuals. Finally, while not every individual in the study showed these effects, they were significant overall. This mixed result should not be misinterpreted to mean that the individuals who enjoyed using the Internet did not suffer any deleterious consequences. Not only was life online correlated for many with a decrease in family relations, a collapsing social life, greater loneliness, and increased depression, these changes also seemed to correlate with a failure of the individuals to recognize these effects as they took place.[11]

This latter point may turn out to be the most significant. As the title, "Internet Paradox," suggests, the gradual effects of going online, whether positive or negative, may not be easily discernible either for the individual or for society. The basic problem is one highlighted earlier in the essay in Part I entitled "Digital Mechanics": there is not likely to be an obvious one-to-one relationship between the use of the technology and its long-term social and psychological effects. Individuals in this particular study may have felt generally worse after one or two years of Internet use, but how easy would it be to pin this on the use of a technology that is said to make life better? And perhaps it was *how* they were using it. Unless one engages in careful self-experimentation, it may not be easy to determine what is the best way to incorporate this technology into one's life in the long run.

In truth, even sophisticated studies such as this are profoundly limited in scope, since they cannot directly assess the larger societal impact of computer and video technology. Let's say, for example, that just the opposite results had been reported in this study, as may be the case in future studies, given that the Internet is becoming a more complete otherworld in which to be entertained, shop, work, socialize, communicate, and find information. Would this be cause for celebration? I hardly think so. If you find great contentment in your virtual life (relative to what's left of your unplugged life), what will this *relative* happiness mean for the rest of us who are not plugged in? Equally important, what will this mean for the overall pursuit of digitopia? If millions of people are finding that an escape into virtuality pays off for them, at least in relative terms, will we build an even more rewarding digital dreamworld to replace the current one?

In the final analysis, I think it will be obvious to most readers that the Internet is not an inherently positive or negative realm of activity for any single individual, but rather depends on myriad other factors. We all know the maxim "It's not technology but how you use it that's important." It's an apt motto, but it addresses the end rather than the beginning of the story. We need to consider not only how the Internet will be used but also how it and all other digital technologies will be used to the exclusion of other activities, especially those in the unplugged world. Is it to be a complement for living an engaged life in the unplugged world (which at this point seems quite doubtful), or is it to be part of the infrastructure for the digital dreamworld called *digitopia*?

VIRTUAL REALITY SHAPES THE MIND IN ITS OWN IMAGE

a psychological theory of why virtuality rules

In the 1936 film *Modern Times,* Charlie Chaplin playfully imitated how people were beginning to move with the rhythm of the new industrial machines. By the end of the millennium, not only had people learned to move with the haste of a silicon chip, they also had come to live in comparison to the pseudorealities of sitcoms and soap operas and daydream in the images of product advertisement. In the digital world of today, we have a whole new array of virtual environments in which to lose ourselves. These digital worlds offer an ever more interactive, dramatic, and hyperreal experience than did their analog predecessors, and as a result, many of us are held within them with even greater force.

The supersession of unmediated reality by virtuality has been, as we have seen, among the primary results. In fact, the advancing digital revolution not only suggests that virtual worlds could one day become an all-encompassing reality, it also ensures that, should such a reality come into being, it would become the one and only reality. For while this final territory of the electronic frontier guarantees an altogether more real artificiality into which to escape, this kind of escape seems to produce—indeed, it requires—a plundering of reality itself. In his book *The Spell of the Sensuous,* the ecologist David Abram speaks of this plundering as regards the natural world:

> Human persons, too, are shaped by the places they inhabit, both individually and collectively. Our body rhythms, our moods, our cycles of creativity and stillness, and even our thoughts are readily engaged and influenced by shifting patterns in the land. Yet our organic attunement to the local earth is thwarted by our ever-increasing intercourse with our own signs. Transfixed by our technologies, we short-circuit the sensorial reciprocity between our breathing bodies and the bodily terrain. Human awareness folds in upon itself, and the senses—once the crucial site of our engagement with the wild and animate earth—become mere adjuncts of an isolate and abstract mind bent on overcoming an organic reality that now seems disturbingly aloof and arbitrary.[1]

In light of the perpetual desire to mediate our experience with technology, two psychological questions arise: First, why would anyone want to flee the unplugged world in the first place, especially given our clear desire to interact socially with others? Second, why does our tendency toward escape from reality have the effect of diminishing the meaning and value of the unplugged world? Even if we assume that you embrace new technologies because they're interesting, useful, enjoyable, or a source of social interaction, this still leaves open the question of why, as these technologies impinge on your experience of the social and the ecological realms, you persist in using them. At first glance, it would appear that why you use them is largely a psychological question concerning human motivation, while the reason we as a society develop them is largely an economic question concerning the profit-driven marketplace. But this is not exactly correct, since these two factors—the economic and the psychological—are really quite intertwined, with each reinforcing the other.

At the core of this dialectic of the individual within society lies a psychological law of diminishing returns. For many, if not most, people, this reanimation of reality begins to unfold as soon as the mind becomes conditioned by virtual worlds more immediately alluring or satisfying than our own.

First, the mind is not some kind of computer that remains unchanged as cultural software runs through its cerebral circuits. Conscious reality changes as the software of everyday life changes, and it remains more or less changed thereafter. Whether it's perusing the glossy ads of *Cosmopolitan,* reading the tabloid media (broadly defined), watching the tube, surfing the Web, playing at PlayStations, or viewing the latest special-effects flick, chronic exposure to simulated ideas and images conditions, albeit to different degrees, your expectations of how the real world should look, how fast it should go, and how you should feel when living in it. Twenty-five years ago, kids forfeited their quarters to a video game called Pong. Pong is to Sony PlayStation 2 what the firecracker is to the atomic bomb. Virtual reality wires us for a virtual world.

Next, as you adapt to the latest digital experiences on offer, straying farther and farther from your home world of the here and now, the real world becomes less satisfying each time you return to it. While technology has always transformed the nature of consciousness by transforming the nature of experience, the digital information age promises to erase every evidence of a boundary between reality and virtuality. Inhabiting stories on the page or screen may or may not fill the mind with ideas and images that, over time, alienate us from the here and now. Alienation becomes nearly certain, however, as virtual technology removes all imagination from our stories and then, going further, removes every awareness that they are only stories. People once packed their picnic baskets and headed for the hills to escape the built world. Today people pack their mobile phones as well—and are bored if they fail to ring. Once people are wired for a virtual world, the present world goes dim.

Finally, as the world fades behind a digital facade, the mind follows. The unmediated world no longer satisfies your digitized needs and wants, thus making virtual worlds more desired destinations. It may be hard to believe that we want to live a totally virtual existence, but as more of us fall out of touch with the old-fashioned world, virtual worlds will begin to appear—and be sold to us—as virtual heavens. Atheists criticized Christians in the past for abandoning the real world for what they saw as an imagined afterlife. Now the quest for Heaven is itself being preempted by the quest for a virtual heaven, encouraging the same abandonment of the here and now. Wired for virtual reality, everyday reality becomes less satisfying, propelling us with even greater momentum toward life in virtual worlds. When virtuality rules, reality sucks.

One question still remains, though, which is why virtual worlds are more immediately alluring or satisfying to us than our own. With more than 200 million TV sets in China today, I would suggest for starters that this has to do with a natural desire we have for indulging the senses with stimulus change—to be distracted, that is, from the everydayness of everyday life. Maybe you're depressed. Maybe you're lonely. Maybe you're not busy and want to be entertained. Whatever the reason, a break from the monotony of everyday life is something that not only spans all the ages—and all classes and races—it also appears to span the species.

In an essay entitled "Primate Peekaboo" the science writer Robert Sapolsky tells us that wild baboons in East Africa like to watch. Naturally, they do not watch everything we watch since they do not have our media technology at hand, nor do they even have the culturally constructed taboos and desires that determine so much of what we like to watch. For example, since the females do not cover their breasts, there's no real tendency toward voyeurism of this sort. However, it turns out that baboons do like spectator sports. Sapolsky reports:

> Bunch of baboons sitting around a field when there's a fight. Two large, high-ranking males, tension has been building up between them over something, and it finally erupts. A hundred pounds of muscle and testosterone, sharpened canines that are bigger than in an adult lion, slashing, lunging, brawling. Someone in the vicinity

might get hurt, either amid the fighting or immediately afterward, with the loser taking out his frustrations on someone smaller. What's the logical thing? Get the hell out of there. And what do half the animals do? Stop what they're doing, stand bipedally, push in closer, all for a better view.[2]

According to Sapolsky, there are many possible reasons for this spectator behavior, but the real reason, he suggests, is that baboons simply like to watch. The implications of this for our own behavior may be minor, but then again, who knows? Perhaps our love of spectacle is in some basic way biological. Perhaps our long journey into digitopia is really a kind of cultural misadventure—a technological explosion set off by a deadly combination: *the capacity to continually create new and more stimulating media technologies and the basic biological bias toward watching that which is, by comparison, more stimulating.* If you doubt this yourself, just think about the last time you were with friends at a bar or restaurant and a television was in view. Even if you detest television in public places, you were probably powerless in your effort not to watch. And as the law of diminishing returns reminds us, watching is the first step.

A DIGITAL VIRUS

how the digital revolution feeds

off a crippled social sphere

The lure of living a virtual existence can be explained only partly by the fact that we like to watch. The desire to inhabit a virtual world—whether to be passively distracted, to play interactively, or to get lost in a narrative story other than your own—emerges out of a larger psychological context that includes the reality of the here and now from which you flee when you go off to watch. In this essay I want to begin discussing this other side of the equation—the unplugged side of the equation—by showing just how much the strength of the digital information age derives from a dying and dysfunctional social sphere.

We know that, as summarized by the psychology of diminishing returns, you are lured into virtual worlds in part because these realms offer something more immediately interesting than the real world around you. We also know that you are lured into virtuality because as you spend more time in the plugged-in world, the capacity of the unplugged world to hold you in its embrace is weakened. The digital rendering of your world promotes a degradation of it, meaning, in other words, that it propels you with even greater momentum into newly minted worlds. Here we see that the need for drama, attention, speed, distraction, newness, and change becomes so inflated that many of the slow and stable parts of your unplugged life can no longer compete with the plugged-in parts. The book that hasn't been read suffers from this. The marriage that hasn't been nourished suffers from this. The house that hasn't been looked after suffers from this. The children who haven't been intimately cared for suffer from this. And when any or all of these things begin to unravel, our tendency is simply to abandon ship: give up reading, get a divorce, sell the house, medicate the child, take refuge in work.[1]

Not only as individuals but also as a society, it seems we are in a downward cycle in which more and more energy is dedicated to building and inhabiting virtual worlds, while the infrastructure of social reality falls to pieces. Kalle Lasn and Bruce Grierson, writing in *Adbusters,* make the point well:

> Skeptics will scoff—*Crisis? What crisis?*—but strip away the intellectualizing, the denial, the vested interest in the myth of sunny, can-do-Americanism, and the intuitive notion persists that something is awry at a fundamental level in many people's lives. It's not so much what that thing is as what it isn't. Something is missing. Something essential and meaningful has been displaced by something . . . less authentic. The possibility that forces outside of our control might be overwhelming us—changing us—is so frightening that most of us busily hunt down safe outlets for the escalating anxiety. We rely in record numbers on prescription drugs. We escape into the media/entertainment pleasureplex. We pile on the amusements only to find (*pace* Leonard Cohen) that "we are locked into our suffering, and our pleasures are the seal."[2]

If social reality is really falling to pieces, the question arises as to what is meant by "social reality." In its optimal form, I believe it to be the following: It is a reality characterized by face-to-face interactions with others with whom one has deeply held commitments. It is, by comparison, not a reality in which most or all social experience is technologically mediated and filtered, where the gestures and expressions of direct human contact are lost. It is also a reality in which we are allowed to be creative and unique—to be individuals—without having to be stripped of the social meaning that comes from living a shared, social existence. It is, by comparison, not a hyperindividualistic reality in which the antisocial norms of society put us at risk for dysfunctional relationships with friends and family, chronic loneliness, dread, and depression. Finally, it is a reality in which you are less psychologically and economically anxious, as your reality is not entrenched in a zero-sum ethos in which one simply tries to eke out what one journalist aptly dubbed in the 1930s "comfortable survival."[3] Pockets of a "self"-sustaining social reality still exist today in America, for example in some tightly knit ethnic communities, but where they do they are almost invariably under siege.

In his acclaimed book *Bowling Alone,* Robert Putnam clarifies the nature of social reality and reports on its health during the second half of the twentieth century. Marshaling a vast array of social science data, Putnam documents in detail the social reality in which the digital age now flourishes. He defines this in terms of the collapse of the American community, the vanishing of social capital, and the disappearance of civic engagement.[4] He tells us that in the past forty or so years, civic life in America has fallen to near-extinction levels. Participating in voluntary organizations, going to dinner parties, to church, and PTA meetings, discussing social issues with neighbors, and voting have all taken a beating in recent decades. Indeed, one reason the picture of civic life a half century ago looks so downright nostalgic is that it stands in such stark contrast with the hasty, hurried, and jacked-in society we so energetically pursue today.

As suggested by the title of his book, Putnam documents, among other things, how the popularity of league bowling increased from the 1930s through the 1960s but has declined ever since. The only major exception to this decline is attendance at live sporting events, though it seems that this has more of an affinity with virtual media such as movies, television, and video games than it does with the active social engagement represented by membership in a bowling league or reading group.

What gives Putnam's bowling example added significance is the fact that the number of bowlers in America is at an all-time high today. Putnam notes, for instance, that while league bowling decreased 40 percent from 1980 to 1993, the number of bowlers in America increased in these years by roughly 10 percent. Bowling is still ostensibly a social affair for millions of Americans, but the disappearance of the bowling league signifies something much more profound, namely, the breakdown of formal social organizations.

Anyone who has participated in bowling leagues or other such groups—or at least has seen the classic Coen brothers film *The Big Lebowski*—knows that the depth and richness of experience cultivated through active membership in social groups often far exceed that which is provided by the spontaneous gathering of informal groups. In the research literature, this is defined in terms of "weak" versus "strong" social ties, the latter of which have been shown to be much more effective, at least historically, in reducing stress and promoting social and psychological well-being.[5] Putnam points out, for example, that "over the last twenty years more than a dozen large studies . . . in the United States, Scandinavia, and Japan have shown that *people who are socially disconnected are between two and five times more likely to die from all causes, compared with matched individuals who have close ties with family, friends, and the community.*"[6] Putnam points out as well that participation in formal organizations teaches us how to live among our fellow men and women. That is, bowling leagues and their ilk teach people how to organize themselves, how to create and build trust with others, and how to inculcate the basic social habits that are essential for any living democracy to work. This seems an all-too-neglected point, for one of the most difficult aspects of "belonging" to anything these days is the sheer incapacity people have for getting along.

In light of these changes, I will go where Putnam obviously fears to tread and suggest that the dramatic increase in psychological problems in the past few decades can be tied directly to this increase in social isolation.[7] The evidence of this includes the following: The prevalence of depression in the United States has gone from about 1 percent at the turn of the century (by age seventy-five) to more than 6 percent today (by age twenty-four); the average age of onset of manic-depression decreased from age thirty-two in the 1960s to age nineteen in the 1990s. In 1999, the *Journal of the American Medical Association* published an extensive analysis of the prevalence of depression worldwide, looking at 39,000 subjects studied in nine epidemiological studies.[8] Among other findings was the discovery that the age of onset of depression has been steadily decreasing with each successive generation throughout this century; this trend was found for the United States as well as for several other nations experiencing social change. Today, nearly one in ten Americans filter their life experiences through antidepressant drugs such as Prozac.

Despite the fact that enduring social networks are essential to human well-being, most people are now disconnected from formal social groups and organizations and, as these data suggest, are reeling from the consequences. With a quarter of all Americans living alone, not only are social relationships becoming more tenuous and superficial, but the sheer amount of social activity—that is, the "social density" of people's lives—is on the decline. Putnam tells us for example that, from the 1970s to 1990s, there was a dramatic decrease in people going out to visit friends as well as having friends over to visit. He summarizes: "Visits with friends are now on the social capital endangered species list. If the sharp, steady declines registered over the *past* quarter century were to continue at the same pace for the *next* quarter century, our centuries-old practice of entertaining friends at home might entirely disappear from American life in less than a generation."[9]

And what are we doing in the meantime? Especially since the birth of the Internet, we are taking the path of least resistance and getting plugged in. And as we have seen, this is no panacea. Studies from the 1990s show, for example, that few individuals develop real friendships through the Web. In the Carnegie Mellon study, which lasted from one to two years for each individual, the making of new friends online was said to be rare, even though these individuals appeared to want to make new friends. Another study showed that even after two or more years on the Internet, only 22 percent of those studied had made a new friend online.[10] Couples trying to keep love alive while living far apart have also turned to using the Internet. One couple who used Webcams to keep in touch daily acknowledged, however, that "even though they felt connected when they were online, they had become lonely as soon as they turned away from the computer."[11] It seems unlikely, in other words, that the loss of density in people's social lives, which is itself correlated with increased risk of depression, will be made up by the fleeting relationships found in cyberspace.

Neither are the negative consequences of jacking in restricted to the social realm. Consider a study published in 2000 in the journal *Diabetes Care.*[12] This study found that from 1990 to 1998, increases in weight gain and adult obesity led to a 33 percent increase in adult-onset (Type 2) diabetes, translating into several million more Americans with diabetes. (From 1991 to '98, the percent of adults defined as obese increased from 12 to 20 percent, which means that diabetes will continue to increase in this century.[13]) Moreover, the greatest increase in Type 2 diabetes was found for younger adults, 30-to-39-year-olds, among whom the increase was 70 percent. What makes this study relevant is the fact that these trends appear to be related to the emerging digital world. A revealing example comes from a *New York Times* columnist: "It was a lovely September afternoon and I was doing what many like-minded souls do on weekends in autumn: playing football with friends. But instead of running around and possibly damaging valuable body parts, I was sitting in a comfortable chair at my friend Jenn Sturm's apartment. I held the video game controller while . . ."[14] An article in *Time* reporting on the diabetes study adds, "Doctors fix at least some of the blame for the growing problem on those other great phenomena of the 1990s: the infatuation with the Internet and the proliferation of cable-TV channels. An increasingly wired country is also becoming an increasingly sedentary one, with Web-surfing kids leading the way."[15]

Meanwhile, with people giving up not just on the realm of social reality but also on their bodies and their health, the plugged-in, bodiless world continues to expand. As Robert Putnam points out, even bowling lanes have adapted by becoming plugged in. In the classic American tradition of "if you can't beat 'em, join 'em," bowling lanes have turned to providing parallel entertainment, employing such things as live rock-'n'-roll bands and big-screen television. This example not only hints at the overall shift toward America becoming a society of spectators, where all doing is gradually transformed into watching, it also documents the degree to which social recreation is being replaced by privatized entertainment. Putnam provides this haunting description of a world gone virtual in *Bowling Alone:*

> The [supreme exaltation] of these trends can be found, most improbably, at the Holiday Bowling Lanes in New London, Connecticut. Mounted above each lane is a giant television screen displaying the evening's TV fare. Even on a full night of league play team members are no longer in lively conversation with one another about the day's events, public and private. Instead each stares silently at the screen while awaiting his or her turn. Even while bowling together, they are watching alone.[16]

This example reminds us that we cannot explain the turn toward virtuality strictly in terms of discrete individual desires or psychological dependencies. Just as virtual technologies act as both cause and effect in our continued advance toward living fully plugged-in lives, the ongoing transformation of human consciousness is both a product of—and a promoter of—global digitization. This means that the relationship between people and digital technology is important for all of society, regardless of how entrenched you are in the digitally enhanced virtual realities of today. For even if you're not a subscriber to the postmodern ethos of "log on, jack in, and drop out," you may still find yourself "watching alone."

FIGHT AND FLIGHT

instead of fighting for a better world,

we're taking flight into virtuality

So how does it feel?
What?
Your real life, the one you came back for?
It feels completely unreal.
You're stuck now, aren't you?

David Cronenberg, eXistenZ

I have suggested the image of us all sitting and watching alone, with everyone on board the same digital information train. This general view, that digital technology shapes the world around us regardless of whether we ourselves embrace it, is nicely captured in the following metaphor for technology, given to us by the Canadian physicist Ursula Franklin:

> [T]echnology has built the house in which we all live. The house is continually being extended and remodeled. More and more of human life takes place within its walls, so that today there is

hardly any human activity that does not occur within this house. All are affected by the design of the house, by the division of its space, by the location of its doors and walls. Compared to people in earlier times, we rarely have a chance to live outside this house. And the house is still changing; it is still being built as well as being demolished.[1]

The metaphor of a house seems appropriate for media technology, and it contrasts well with the metaphor of social reality as a woven fabric. As we have seen, media can shelter us like a house, and they can be demolished and then replaced with even more elaborate ones, creating what we have today: a media estate. But no matter how elaborate the estate, it cannot really warm our existence the way the social fabric can—up close, worn tightly, and formed over time to our own particular shape and size.

In pointing to the loss of traditional sources of meaning in everyday life (and the rise of what I believe to be inferior alternatives in today's hyperculture), I want to stress again that my principal concern is not economic or political but rather psychological. Without question, it's clear that the fabric of social reality has been torn apart in the last century, with our thoughts and actions driven by the imperatives of an increasingly individualistic social order. As this has taken place, we have not sought to repair the tears in the social fabric. We have attempted instead to adapt at the individual level—a kind of (mal)adaptation that just happens to fit the offerings of "lifestyle" capitalism.[2] As the psychologist Philip Cushman has shown, millions of Americans have come to respond to the meaninglessness of modern life by forever trying to fill up "the empty self" with material goods.[3] Another critic writes: "We have no life, only 'lifestyle'—an abstraction of life, based on the sacred symbolism of the Commodity."[4] Writing in a similar vein, the British psychologist Oliver James points out:

A sharp rise in aspirations and individualism since 1950, necessary for continuous economic growth, has led to an all-consuming preoccupation with our status, power and wealth relative to others. We compare ourselves obsessively, enviously and self-destructively, thus corrupting the quality of our inner lives. No sooner than we achieve a goal, we move the goalposts to create a new, more difficult one, leaving ourselves permanently dissatisfied and depleted, always yearning for what we have not got, a nation of Wannabees.[5]

This much is not new and seems to me hardly debatable in today's "low serotonin society."[6] This does, however, bring us back to a central argument of the book. As the utopian dream of the consumer society has failed to materialize—in large part because it was exploitative of the breakdown in the social production of meaning in our lives—the disappearance of a strong social reality has been accompanied by an attendant buildup of virtual realities that substitute for it. Realizing this, you can see why digital technologies have an almost erotic lure today, given how they represent in the American mind a fusing of the social with the technological. With every social encounter becoming enclosed within a glowing electronic circuitry, we see the digital future as pregnant with a new kind of virtual community. This will be a perfect world in which all individuals are isolated within their own physical space, capable of jacking in and out of relationships at will—no responsibility, no commitment, no requirement of a stable or honest identity. Evidence of this naive, utopian outlook is common in the hype concerning the Internet. It's also represented in the rapid buildup of mediated social networks and chat rooms on the Web, the vast number of online romances that have materialized in recent years, and the rapid adoption of mobile phones and other wireless communication devices.

There is, however, a serious problem with this technoromantic vision. The filtering of social relations through a data stream of ones and zeros seems to strip vital nutrients from our social experiences, leaving us with a means that literally opposes its intended ends. As is suggested by most research on the Internet, the result is little more than a further plundering of the social realm. Meanwhile, as social reality disappears behind the shadow of an emerging digital matrix, you are apt to feel as though you have little choice but to continue to search for meaning in cyberspace, or at least head there in the hope of escaping the increasing stress and meaninglessness of your life in the unplugged world. A cycle is thus formed that is like that of any cycle of addiction, where the stimulus that satisfies the need ultimately creates an even greater one.

What this ultimately means for us today is that we are caught in *the middle years.* These are the years in which you find yourself suspended between two opposing worlds, the outer world of society and nature and the interior world of simulated reality. The former represents earlier times, when people lived lives deeply embedded within the facticity of nature and community. The latter represents future times, when you will live a life of total abandonment, embedded in a sea of technologies so all-encompassing that, as pure extensions of yourself, they will be invisible. Thus, rather than living blissfully in one of these singular worlds, whether real or virtual, you are split torturously across two. The result is that millions of people are trying with great energy and fanfare to fuse social and virtual reality together, not by going out and fighting for a new and stronger concrete reality that can nourish our minds and bodies, but by fleeing into a virtual reality that, as we have seen, leaves the body behind. Let's consider two examples more closely: e-mail and chat rooms.

In the 1999 film *Cruel Intentions,* a young man is seeking clandestine correspondence with a young woman whose parents despise him. He laments to a friend, "I don't even know her e-mail address." To this the friend responds, "E-mail is for geeks and pedophiles," advising him to woo her instead with letters.

In the past half decade, electronic correspondence has largely supplanted what remained of written correspondence. Many retired letter writers have even convinced themselves that e-mail has single-handedly resurrected the lost art of letter writing. But has it really? You might, upon checking your personal mail each day, expect to find in it ads, bills, perhaps even a check. Your name and address handwritten on the envelope of a personal letter come as a delightful surprise; the idiosyncrasies of the script, the stationery, and even the stamp art charm you and endear the sender to you. For some time afterward, you savor the sensual experience of rereading the letter—its look, texture, and scent—and afterward treasure it as a nostalgic memoir, a footnote to one's personal history.

When we log in to our e-mail server, the expectation of finding new mail negates any possible excitement or surprise; if there's no new mail, we're disappointed. Although linguistically an e-mail can carry the same message as a letter, the two media have different effects on our consciousness. The intangibility of e-mail, its existence—or, rather, nonexistence—only as bits of information stored somewhere on a magnetic hard drive and viewed on a computer screen, gives it an ephemeral quality that creates a shallower impression on the mind. Simply, an e-mail is quickly forgotten. Correspondence via e-mail is handy, but does "getting in touch" not become banal as a result? One wonders, I suppose, if the same will apply to e-books.

While virtual letters are supplanting real letters, the art of live conversation too is becoming "virtually" nonexistent. Throughout the plugged-in world, lonely men and women log in to chat zones in search of new friends, acquaintances, and lovers. Seeking solace in technological immersion—having abandoned any hope of creating and maintaining relationships within our own community—we are turning to the Internet as an online, digital village. The automobile, the suburb, the television—all have been instrumental in tearing down community and promoting isolation. For many, logging in to a chat room seems the ideal escape. Indeed, within certain circumscribed sets of conditions, where off-line culture offers no real community, online culture may. But this too is illusion.

Personalized webpages replete with photos, opinions, and biographical information pander to a culture of hyperindividualism—virtual shrines to the virtual self.[7] Here the collectivity of community is lost in a mosaic of individual egos, each seeking fulfillment from others, yet putting little at risk in return. Web-based marriages? Maybe. Web-based divorces? Certainly. While many online affairs go off-line with people traveling cross-country or across borders to shack up with NICEGUY2000 or EASYs123, the virtual solution reveals, just as it promotes, the continuing collapse of social relationships and community in the unplugged world. While the human need for companionship might be momentarily satisfied by these ersatz relationships, one doubts whether spending one's evenings in a swivel chair, eyes glued to a glowing screen, can really fill the empty self. As Robert Wright has argued, "The problem is that too little of our 'social' contact is social in the natural, intimate sense of the word."[8]

What, then, might we contrast to the ephemeral pursuits of the virtual self? The only real possibility is the sensuous world that lies behind the digital curtain, where human engagement occurs in real time and real space. This is not necessarily a world in which you *must* live in order to survive as a mental being, but it's the one and only world in which you *can* thrive as a social being. Here you find a lost world of extended, unmediated, and uninterrupted social exchanges with friends and loved ones, of reading and writing, of bicycling and walking, of playing sports, gardening, creating works of art, traveling, being outdoors. This is, in other words, a world of engagement where human contentment comes about as you become engrossed in sustained, meaningful activities well suited to your interests and capacities.[9]

In pointing out the obvious, however, I do not mean to suggest that the sensual and the virtual are mutually exclusive worlds. To the contrary, it's because they are overlapping worlds that your sensibilities can be conditioned in one—the "virtual"—and then disappointed in another—the "real." Psychological, socioeconomic, and historical forces are encouraging flight over fight, which they do today with almost complete impunity.

THE DRAMA OF
THE DIGITAL SELF

no more struggle between the will to power

and the need for mutual recognition

Thus far I have attempted to throw some light on the question of reality versus virtuality, and to suggest some reasons why the digital revolution has encouraged and will continue to encourage a flight from the former and into the latter. In doing this, I have examined how being jacked in changes who we are, with the result that we are gradually becoming better adapted for these artificial worlds than we are for our own. I have also examined how the social reality that would normally compete against this flight into virtuality is failing to do so. An important reason is that, with the individualism of our society so perfectly interfaced with plugged-in realities, social reality and the self have become malnourished. People are less actively involved in formal social groups while at the same time more passively engaged in relationships of another kind—that is, relationships with technology. The fact that there has been so little public concern over this trend is disturbing, especially when we consider its power to perpetuate itself. Being stripped naked of our social clothing pushes us toward escape into virtuality, and escape tears away what's left of our social clothing. By offering a refuge for our naked selves, virtual reality encourages a flight from everyday reality and thus a further abandonment of the here and now.

In this essay, I shall attempt to provide a more thoroughgoing psychological account of our flight into virtuality, which I do by exploring the drama of the digital self. By using the term "drama" I mean to suggest that our relationship to the social world is much more complex than is captured in the commonplace idea that we are social animals. A much more accurate and useful view has been articulated by various psychological writers and researchers, all of whom can be loosely grouped under the heading of "self psychology" or "object relations theory."

This school of thought has described how, throughout human history, each individual self has come to live in suspension between the outwardness of social reality and the inwardness of a closed-off private self. Life is, in other words, a drama between two opposing extremes, the extreme of pure selflessness and the extreme of pure selfishness. Neither of these extremes, if embraced, can meet your basic psychological needs. For example, writing on the subject of domination in relationships, Jessica Benjamin notes in *The Bonds of Love* that "domination and submission result from a breakdown of the necessary tension between self-assertion and mutual recognition that allows self and other to meet as sovereign equals."[1] By comparison, finding a healthy balance between these two poles— self-assertion and mutual recognition—is the source of all positive social reality, and thus when people's paths are not blocked, they naturally pursue some kind of truce between themselves and the social world. Not only does this drama take many paths, these paths are traveled throughout your life. You may go through periods in which this truce sometimes favors inclusiveness and other periods when it favors exclusiveness.

Although it may not be immediately obvious, this concept has great import in these digital times. With the construction of a fully wired (and wireless) world under way, the digital revolution is tipping the balance in this drama, and in a destructive direction. No longer are you essentially forced to try to find your place in the outer, social world; you can simply turn away from it and inhabit a virtual one instead. There is no clearer case, I think, than that of a discontented adolescent who escapes from reality through the cyberspace portal located in his or her bedroom (an image that contrasts sharply with the imaginary world that a child might invent within the enclosed space of his or her wardrobe). Here, as in the oft-cited example of the Columbine High students Dylan Klebold and Eric Harris, individuals are free to drift out of the reality of their immediate environment and into another reality. As the Klebold/Harris example illustrates, this escapist reality is likely to feed their sense of boredom, isolation, and alienation, thus antagonizing rather than promoting a productive stance in the world beyond the bedroom door.

The original insight behind human development as a "drama" between self and other comes from observations of the earliest stages of infant development. It's here we see that individuals are not inherently predestined for strong and healthy social relationships. Instead, an infant human comes into the world with a complete and utter sense of oneness. All the world is her, or him; not her world or his world, but the world *as* her or *as* him. There are no relationships at this stage because there is nothing—no object, no other, no world—with which to have a relationship. Obviously, this is not a social approach to the world, but rather a wholly antisocial approach. And, as noted, taking such a stance in the world will not work. As time passes, the known universe of the infant expands, while at the same time the caregiver(s) begins to desire a greater independence from the child. Here arises a profound drama between self and other.

On the one hand, the child wishes to stay fused with the world, to reject the idea that there is a universe of objects independent of oneself that the child must negotiate rather than dominate. On the other hand, the continued refusal to break from this oneness causes increasing misery for the child, since the mother and others refuse to accept this egotistical stance any longer. By this I mean that parents and siblings gradually begin to expect some recognition of their own, disturbing the child's sense of oneness and thus putting pressure on the child to break out of his or her self-centeredness. This is a natural and unconscious process for all parties.

This renegotiation, or "hatching out" as it has often been called, is a hugely important psychological process. As a lifelong motion in people's lives, it has been well described in books such as Robert Kegan's *The Evolving Self* and Alice Miller's *The Drama of the Gifted Child.*[2] As these psychologists have made clear, the kinds of social relationships that infuse your life with durable and lasting meaning are not simply donated to you as you enter the world, but rather are—if they are at all—negotiated over the course of your life. Through families, neighborhoods, and communities, social reality has evolved into a supporting web that people weave together over time, creating collective social structures of various shapes and sizes. These structures then support each new generation of youths as they are pushed out into the world, forced into a truce with an immediate social reality that both challenges and supports their existence as selves.

The natural drama of the self in the social world unfolds in a very different way for the digital self. And here we can draw a conclusion that I think needs to be emphasized above all others: *In place of strong social structures that support a balance between inclusiveness and exclusiveness in the material world, we now have strong technological structures that support an imbalance in favor of hyperexclusiveness.* This situation is already quite apparent and will become even more so as the digital revolution marches on. Consequently, in the digital near future we will be looking less at a unified "evolving self" who feels pulled into and held by the social world, and more at a fragmented "devolving self" who, having found the social world to be an unsustaining psychological space, is lured back into a privatized world suspended in virtuality.

We are, in other words, moving toward a time when the very structure of society—postmodern society—is tailored to accommodating and reinforcing the needs of what R. D. Laing called the "divided self."[3] Most selves today are not so disturbed as to fall into a schizophrenic condition, but millions of people are becoming divided selves in that they are losing what Laing identifies as a sense of substantiality—that is, a sense of being a unified individual who is aware of his or her own continuity over time.

The discontented adolescent who escapes into cyberspace is by no means the only example to which we can point. In fact, people are escaping into virtuality at every level of social interaction. There's the discontented wife who, to escape her marriage, goes online in search of new mates. There's the harried parent who, to keep a child occupied at home or in the car, plugs him in. There's the discontented employee who, to rebel against the workplace, stays jacked in all day at work. All this is summed up well in a TV advertisement in which the father hails the virtues of Internet shopping for the wife, the television and the cordless phone for the adolescent daughter, and video games for the younger children. With all this, the father tells us, he can finally get some peace and quiet.

Examples such as these do not just suggest that everyone is jacking in and dropping out. They also suggest how the lure of the digital domain undermines the fundamental tension that makes enduring social relationships possible. A boy writing an e-mail to his grandmother is a nice image, I suppose, but not if this behavior serves as a substitute for doing what the boy really doesn't want to do, which is visit his grandmother. And this hurts not only the grandmother; if the boy takes the path of least resistance, he will miss the chance of developing a meaningful and perhaps enduring relationship with his elders.

All this raises another question about our race toward the digital future: What happens to social reality when the needed internal pressures that frame it have been blown out through a portal into cyberspace? The situation we thus face is not unlike that of an astronaut, wondering whether one's integrity can be maintained in a world of zero gravity. When even the slightest social tension causes us to shoot off into cyberspace, how can we possibly continue to build, at the psychological, social, or political level, a reality worth living in?

DIGITAL DREAMS, CONCRETE REALITIES

how the desires of the plugged-in world

spill over into everyday life

In the Greek myth of Narcissus, a young man falls in love with an image reflected in a pool (the image is his, although he does not know it) and afterward wastes away from unfulfilled desire. If Narcissus were alive today, however, he could not simply fall in love with his own image. Instead, he would have to fall in love with an idealized, digitally enhanced image of himself. For in the emerging digital world of today, reality lives, to the extent that it lives at all, in the reflection of hyperreality. Whether Narcissus, Michael Jackson, or just plain old you, *the real thing* is no longer that with which one falls in love. Call it love or call it lust, today we are in want of that which is more real than real, more natural than natural, more human than human. And thus it's no wonder that, like Narcissus, we are unable to find happiness in the abundance of our day. For there can be no satisfying a lust for impossible dreams.

There can also be no grasping our lust for impossibilities without first recognizing our long journey into digitopia. As we have seen, media technology has, over the millennia, built an impressive stage on which to lose ourselves in stories, and many people today have little interest in leaving it. There is no conspiracy here, just a process of cultural evolution marching toward ultimate control over every force and facet of nature, reality included, and at whatever cost. In some places this has happened sooner (America) rather than later (China), but there can be no doubt that in the global information age, it's happening everywhere.

Around the world, wherever people are experiencing the razing of their social reality, mental health is on the decline. As Arthur Kleinman and Alex Cohen of Harvard Medical School wrote in *Scientific American* in 1997, "Behind this rise in the prevalence of mental illness [in countries such as India and China] is an array of demographic and social factors. . . . Rapid urbanization, chaotic modernization and economic restructuring have left many developing countries reeling."[1] Closer to home are the findings reported in a study published in 1999 in the *Archives of General Psychiatry*.[2] Examining the prevalence of psychological dysfunction in Mexican Americans, researchers found that both Mexicans and recent Mexican immigrants in the United States had half the risk of suffering from depression, anxiety, and drug addiction as Mexican Americans who had either been born in the United States or who had lived in the United States for more than thirteen years (the latter rates of psychological dysfunction were the same as those measured for other Americans).

Why does life in America make people sick, especially considering its fantastic wealth and opportunity compared with most other parts of the world? One reason is that the American dream, embodied today in terms of consumer capitalism, is itself toxic. As William Leach, writing in *Land of Desire,* notes, "Market capitalism *was* hostile; no immigrant culture—and, to a considerable degree, no religious tradition—had the power to resist it, as none can in our own time. Any group that has come to this country has had to learn to accept and to adjust to this elemental feature of American capitalist culture."[3] In other words, the Mexicans got what they wanted—the American dream—but lost what they had.

American psychological woes also stem in part from the related fact that, more than any other nation (and certainly much more than a nation such as Mexico), the United States has been steadfast in its privileging of technological solutions over social ones. Not only have these technological "solutions" failed to create a more humane society, they have in fact often led to other, secondary social problems. This problem is summarized by Neil Postman in *Technopoly:* "Stated in the most dramatic terms, the accusation can be made that the uncontrolled growth of technology destroys the vital sources of our humanity. It creates a culture without a moral foundation. It undermines certain mental processes and social relations that make human life worth living. Technology, in sum, is both friend and enemy."[4]

Finally, I think this sickness stems from the fact that life in America has been continually narrowed down to three roles, all of which define the individual in brutal economic terms: worker, consumer, and patient. Americans are working more than ever (both men and women), they are shopping more than ever, and they are taking more psychotropic drugs than ever.[5] Is there an interlocking relationship among these three roles? Do they mutually reinforce one another to the exclusion of other roles? I think they do. The monopolization of our time by work leaves us stressed and incapacitated, and destroys our capacity to cultivate other realms of meaningful activity, whether social (e.g., meeting friends one evening a week for dinner) or nonsocial (e.g., painting or gardening). As this takes place, we fall into the role of passive consumers, spending our time and money shopping, Web surfing, and watching. Relating this to the hypercapitalism in America—"where 12 billion display ads, three million radio commercials and 200,000 TV commercials are dumped into the collective subconscious daily"[6]—Richard Wainwright notes, "When advertisers fill our consciousness with images of beautiful, happy, one-dimensional people, they feed the illusion that our innate dissatisfaction can be relieved by material acquisitions. By stuff."[7] (Note that a drug company is now seeking Food and Drug Administration approval to market a Prozac-like drug, Celexa, for the "treatment" of compulsive shoppers.)[8]

The net effect of inhabiting these roles to the exclusion of others— for example, the roles of parent, lover, friend, neighbor, teammate, mentor, citizen, volunteer—is that we don't feel so well. The problem today takes one of two forms, both of which reflect our being caught in the middle years of the digital age. First, millions of people's lifestyles represent maladaptive strategies for coping in a world that is fundamentally antagonistic to people's well-being. Second, even those individuals whose lives are reasonably intact still find themselves struggling to achieve a sense of inner peace and well-being. This latter problem is because of the relative nature of psychological contentment—that is to say, our lives often fall far short of the images and expectations we have acquired for what life should be like.

You walk down the street, look at the trees, the houses, the sky, and say, "I am here, I inhabit a real world with real people and real experiences. The world still exists, and I still live in it." Yet think of all the places your mind has been and all the moments in history that, via simulation, you have experienced. What is the consequence of sharing your mind with so many virtual spaces and experiences? As research on memory now shows, there is no reason to believe that the desires of the plugged-in world will not spill over and contaminate everyday life.

Memories of past experiences, whether real or virtual, are not isolated in separate compartments that can be opened and closed at will.[9] In fact, the whole idea of discrete memories is very misleading. Past experience alters the neural relationships among brain cells in such a way that any single memory relies on neural connections that are also involved in the experience of other memories. This means that the memory of real events can overlap with your memories of simulated events, as has been made clear in studies in which people show a blending together of memories associated with firsthand experience and those that are socially and technologically constructed.[10] Jay Chiat, a self-proclaimed advertising guru, aptly describes the result in an essay entitled "Illusions Are Forever":

> Advertising—including movies, TV, and music videos—presents to us a world that is not our world but rather a collection of images and ideas created for the purpose of selling. These images paint a

picture of the ideal family, the perfect home. What a beautiful woman is, and is not. A prescription for being a good parent and a good citizen. . . . The power of these messages lies in their unrelenting persuasiveness, the 24-hour-a-day drumbeat that leaves no room for an alternative view. We've become acculturated to the way advertisers and other media-makers look at things, so much so that we have trouble seeing things in our own natural way. Advertising robs us of the most intimate moments in our lives because it substitutes an advertiser's idea of what ought to be.[11]

Leave it to an advertising executive to know the truth about reality—or rather the lie that has become the truth. By including such things as movies, television, and music videos in the circle of advertising, Chiat encourages here a radical view of all mass media, implying that everything from the nightly news to TV biographies is constructed first and foremost as self-advertisement. These media are programmed not to challenge the status quo or even the mind but simply to sell themselves. They are entertainment through and through.

While this conditioning begins with the influence of mass media, it also disperses, like toxic waste seeping into the soil, poisoning people for generations to come. As I illustrated earlier with the example of women's sense of body image, it's clear that in some general and not necessarily conscious way, girls and women come to acquire a sense of their appearance from others—siblings, friends, parents, boyfriends, strangers—combined with the constant bombardment of media images. Exactly the same phenomenon applies to the more general problem of trying to find contentment in one's life. The idea that how you view the world affects your sense of well-being is often interpreted to mean that if you would just look at things rationally, you would be well again. But this misses the point. The question is not whether you are happy but just don't know it; the question is whether you have been conditioned in such a way that an interpretive lens of experience is now deeply embedded within your psyche that makes you prone to becoming depressed.

In pointing the finger at mass media—by which I mean advertisements, books, magazines, film, television, video games, and other facets of popular culture—I acknowledge that these trends have been under way for some time. In fact, like Marshall McLuhan, the historian Daniel Boorstin had already identified the most pernicious effects of mass media by the early 1960s, noting at the time that we had fallen deeply into a web of illusions about what reality really has to offer. "We want and we believe these illusions because we suffer from extravagant expectations," he wrote. "We expect too much of the world. Our expectations are extravagant in the precise dictionary sense of the word—'going beyond the limits of reason or moderation.' They are excessive."[12] Of course Boorstin's warnings about the perils of a society trapped in illusion were not heeded, and the dominance of the virtual world has since grown beyond anything Boorstin could have imagined at the time.

As a result, the "lifestyle" approach to everyday life has become the norm, relegating people to the narrow economic roles of worker, consumer, and patient. To wit: the social and technological construction of desire has not just become normative, it has become a "necessary" ingredient in maintaining our all-important economic growth.

The lifestyle approach is in fact so much the norm today that the reader may well be asking: As opposed to what? This is a question I explore more in Part IV, but let me anticipate a bit by suggesting a metaphor that distinguishes between two different approaches—the metaphor of depth. The lifestyle approach represents an essentially nomadic relationship with the world, where all is surface and motion, where history disappears, and where the prime motivation in life is the sheer quantity of experience that one consumes. In contrast to this is the approach of the everyday local citizen, whose relationship is based on depth and permanence, and for whom the quality of experience is paramount.[13] Both these approaches have an almost infinite reach in the world—one deep down and one across the surface—although what is grasped for and acquired in each case is dramatically different.

FEELING OH, SO ANALOG
IN AN ALL-TOO-DIGITAL AGE

why faster computers and better graphics

will never be enough

The psychological theory of adaptation introduced earlier suggests how virtual worlds shape the mind in their own image. The previous essay examined this in terms of desire, suggesting that American culture is not just media-driven, it's driven by a mass media that captures you in a spell of hyperreality, thereby contaminating the meaning and value of the unplugged world. Life in the digital age will of course mean a further expansion of this trend, such that we now have children being exposed to commercial capitalism in the classroom—a trend that is the product of the incorporation of television, video, and computer media into both public and private schools.[1]

In the following two essays we will look at these questions further. This essay looks at people's growing need for speed, while the following one looks at our ever-abbreviated attention span and how we accommodate ourselves by living a distracted way of life. This is followed by the last essay of Part III, which links these symptoms of hyperculture to the pharmacological aid that has become so popular in these middle years.

In my first book, *Ritalin Nation: Rapid-Fire Culture and the*

Transformation of Consciousness, I explored in detail how American culture has sped up over the past two centuries, creating what I called "sensory addictions."[2] I will not review this history here, but I do suggest this earlier work to anyone who is interested in the relationship among cultural history, lifestyle, one's perception of time and space, and the behavioral comportment of ourselves and our children or grandchildren.

In this essay, I want to focus on how the digital age relates to my earlier findings in *Ritalin Nation,* with the hope of clarifying why faster (and faster) computers and better (and better) graphics will never be enough to satisfy our technological urges. In explaining why you are apt to feel oh, so analog in this all-too-digital age, I also hope to clarify further why you fail to recognize just how virtual your life has become and will continue to become as the digital information age rolls on. The short answer is this: just as you adapt to the drama, romance, and excitement you experience in virtual worlds, you also adapt to the rhythm and realism that these worlds provide. This means that, as the psychology of diminishing returns suggests, time spent in virtuality actually compresses and dims our experience of unplugged reality, thus reinforcing the cycle of addiction identified earlier.

To illustrate, consider video-game consoles such as Sony's new PlayStation 2 or Sega's Dreamcast. These multimedia devices are dramatically more powerful than their predecessors, which include everything from Pong to Atari to the original Nintendo. Given their phenomenal power, we might ask whether this latest technology will really "supercharge interactive entertainment" and "catapult a thriving game-console industry into another galaxy," as a *Newsweek* article has suggested for PlayStation 2.[3] The fact that this same hype has been applied to each new generation of video-game technology should tell us that the answer is no. The reason is that the mind has a natural tendency to adapt to the latest speed and realism, such that what looks fantastically faster and more realistic one moment becomes the normative experience the next. By "normative experience" I mean that once this honeymoon period is over, which may last only a few days or weeks, the "wow" power of the technology returns to essentially the same level as for the last generation of technology (and so on, back to the original video games). Each new generation of hardware does only one thing that's permanent: it makes the previous one obsolete. Writing on the video-game industry, Paul Keegan explains:

> Will the most gruesome games of today become so commonplace that they'll eventually elicit nothing more than a bored yawn? . . . Sony, Nintendo, and Sega . . . are not spending billions of dollars to create clever story lines. They are competing madly with one another to create the fastest video-game console ever, each boasting more horsepower than some of the most powerful supercomputers packed just 10 years ago.[4]

If you don't believe this, just ask yourself whether your children really enjoy or appreciate their current video-game equipment more than they did their first video games. If this doesn't apply to you, you might instead ponder the history of film. While the first viewers of motion pictures actually responded to them as real, producing an effect of this nature today requires something like an IMAX theater, and even then the effect is not as dramatic. As noted in Part I, this was aptly captured in a remark by Phil Tippett about the 1925 film *The Lost World:* "If you read the reviews of *Lost World,* the critics back then were ecstatic—they couldn't believe it! They thought the filmmakers must have gone into the South American plateaus to shoot real dinosaurs! My kids watch the movie today and say 'My God!—it looks like they were made of papier-mâché and clay!' "[5] Again, we adapt to the latest speed and realism, always needing something newer and faster to get our kicks, or to feed our growing need for speed.

At this point you may have noticed what seems like a contradiction. If you naturally adapt to the realism and rhythm that the latest in media technology provide, how can it be that virtual worlds are becoming increasingly attractive havens in which to flee from the unplugged world? If you adapt to your electronic experiences, in other words, why would anything be more attractive than what came before them? This is not only a legitimate question, it's also a question that illuminates a crucial aspect of our general pursuit of digitopia.

As just noted, when the virtual domain becomes more interactive, more realistic, and more accelerated, we accommodate to those changes such that they become the new standard of what's needed to meet one's newly inflated sensory expectations. Meanwhile, the unplugged world remains the same. Put these two facts together and we are back to the law of diminishing returns: as virtual worlds become hyperreal, the old-fashioned world fades in comparison to the new standard—regardless of how fast, how real, how dramatic, or how romantic the experience might be.

Thus, for the virtual realm, the point isn't that graphics are more lifelike than ever before but that they have to be—*and they will always have to continue to be*—if they are to seem anything more than ordinary. For the unplugged realm, moreover, the point isn't that the latest virtuality is experienced as so dramatic or spellbinding relative to the past, but that the unplugged world is all the less dramatic and spellbinding as a result. Media technologies do not bring great things to life, they simply shift the venue where you have to go to feel alive.

But why do we fail to see this transfer of power taking place, given how pervasive it is in the world around us? As has been suggested, part of the reason is that we tend to treat our experiences in the hyperreal world as the standard while ignoring the ways in which the standard continues to change. We see 1970s TV programming and immediately realize how dated it has become. What most of us do not do is recognize what this reveals about how the nature of reality—both virtual reality and real virtuality—is changing.

Part of the explanation for this also has to do with the faith we have in the power of technology to speed things up and thus slow us down, which technology supposedly does by giving us more free time. Of course, for most anyone engaged in the digital world of computers, video games, wireless communication, and so on, just the opposite occurs: when you look at the actual impact plugged-in technology has on your consciousness, you see that technology actually speeds *you* up and slows *things* down. As with the example above regarding television, you're apt to overlook the ways in which technology changes the nature of experience. What used to be fast is now experienced as slow, and even those who used to go slowly now go faster and faster.

Adapting this to the law of diminishing returns, we end up with five steps. First, as things speed up and intensify, you adapt to the new level of incoming stimulation, such that what once was stimulating no longer is. Second, as this occurs, you experience something called "protracted duration," in which time seems to be stretched out or slowed down under conditions of waiting or slowness. Third, you require even more intense stimulation to "feel" stimulated rather than bored. Fourth, to meet this demand, you then go faster and buy what's faster, but this only promotes a further sense of protracted duration and thus creates still greater sensory needs. And five, the final result occurs as more and more realms of the unplugged world become too boring or slow, with you turning to still newer technologies to speed them up.

The implications of this process of temporal compression are great. With research showing that American children are spending significantly more time engaged in plugged-in technologies indoors, and significantly less time engaged in unplugged activities outdoors, we have to wonder about what is happening to their sense of time and space.[6] Might there be an unbridgeable chasm growing, in other words, between the slowness that comes from, say, reading a book, and the acceleration that comes from, say, playing a video game or surfing the Web? Are more and more children incapable of sitting still and paying attention because the unplugged world is becoming too slow for their adapted, or "sensory-addicted," minds? It seems to me that children and adults alike are less likely to read, write, draw, practice a musical instrument, or build things with their hands for this reason—that is, they have less capacity to transition into, and inhabit, the psychological spaces in which slowness occurs.

Of course, not all of this is a result of people playing video games. Temporal compression and protracted duration also apply in the adult realm with computers. When you first plug in a newer and faster machine, you experience the intoxication of the accelerated speed. You then adapt to it after a short period. And then you suffer from it forevermore, for now the experience of waiting for minutes has been compressed down to seconds. With a sense of protracted duration firmly in place, impatience that used to arrive only after minutes of waiting, if at all, now arrives after only seconds.

And this does not apply just to the stimulation you bring upon yourself. Consider the bombardment of your senses from uninvited sources. To tickle your brain or get your attention, moviemakers, television producers, advertisers, retailers, and manufacturers all know the secret of sensory addiction, where more stimulation is always needed—and always sells.[7] To take one example, you might recall a TV advertisement for the George W. Bush presidential campaign that showed the word "rats" on the small screen for one thirtieth of a second. This provoked a storm of criticism, with pundits asking whether the Republicans were resorting to transmitting subliminal messages. What does this have to do with the idea that speed sells? Well, when the individual in charge of producing the ad was asked why this flashing of words had been used, he stated that it had nothing to do with subliminal messages but rather was an attempt to create what the industry calls a "visual drumbeat" that ensures that viewers become "interested and involved."

With the mind constantly adapting to a sensory world competing for what little is left of your shrinking attention span, a visual drumbeat is about all that will work, though not for long.

THE INCREDIBLE SHRINKING
ATTENTION SPAN

how you accommodate yourself to a
distracted way of life

Time has become the new commodity—the scarcity of which is
conspicuously displayed as a sign of status.

Daniel Schorr[1]

I have said much thus far about how digital technology takes you a
revolutionary step forward in your capacity to take flight from reality. You may have noticed, however, that many of the popular digital devices on offer today do not actually transport you to another
world. Or do they? Laptop computers, Discmans, wireless e-mail,
mobile phones, PDAs and other handheld devices, and wearable
computers—these sorts of devices may not catapult you into another place and time, but they do serve much the same psychological function by distracting you from yourself. As suggested in the
previous essay, in the electronic age the mind is constantly adapting
to a cluttered and sensory-saturated world that competes nonstop for
what little attention span is left. In this essay I want to show that,

as a result, people are now busier than ever accommodating them-selves to a distracted way of life.[2]

Viewed in literal terms, a shrunken attention span means that the brain has itself become accommodated to a distracted way of life. Neuroscientists now know that nerve cells, or neurons, in the mam-malian brain—at least those that deal specifically with attention and discrimination—are stingy. By this I mean that there are mas-sive numbers of neurons in the brain that will fire up the conscious mind only under certain, ecologically relevant conditions. As should be obvious from an evolutionary point of view, there is an advantage in having a brain that can discriminate that which is im-portant from that which is not, and without requiring the organ-ism's full attention. The ecological world contains a vast amount of stimuli, and there is no way for any organism to attend to it all, let alone sort out all the meaningful chunks of information. As a result, animals' nervous systems have acquired the capacity to ignore most of what's in the environment while still paying attention to that which is significant (which usually has to do with hunting or self-preservation). At the same time, however, it's not always cer-tain what will and will not be important, and thus it's better if this ability to discriminate is a general one, leaving it up to personal ex-perience to determine those things to which an organism does and does not need to pay attention.

To give an example, researchers measuring the activity of spe-cific neurons in the brains of monkeys have found that neurons that fire to the presentation of novel stimuli quickly learn to cease firing if these stimuli do not carry any additional meaning with them. In other words, if these stimuli must be perceived in order for the ani-mal to acquire food, the neurons will continue to stimulate the higher levels of attention and perception in the brain; if they do not, this activity will cease to take place. What actually happens is quite dramatic. When the stimuli are neither novel nor important, certain neurons in the brain actually begin to fire in such a way as to shut down the activity of other neurons, thus keeping the latter from ac-tivating higher brain processes. Some neural groups fire to create attention and perception, while others fire to shut down attention and perception, all of which is tied to a learning process that is highly sensitive to the workings of the ecological world. For humans, the "cocktail-party" effect is a good example. This occurs in situations where, when surrounded by a hundred voices, your brain lights up when it hears someone say your name. When irrelevant names are spoken, you can rest assured that certain neurons in your brain are keeping other neurons from bringing these names to your attention.

What does this process of habituation mean, then, for the incredible shrinking attention span? First and foremost, it means that the human brain that finds itself submerged in a world of constant stimulation will become a brain that attends to only the most alluring stimuli in the environment. Stimuli that cannot rise above the threshold of our media-laden environment may not only fail to be effective in getting and maintaining your attention, they may simply fail to reach the level of consciousness. This especially applies to stimuli in the unplugged world, such as those provided by a book's print, a teacher's words, or street signs at the side of the road.

While a blind person becomes hypersensitized to the meaning available in other sources of stimulation provided by the environment (e.g., sound), a sensory-saturated person becomes hyper*de*sensitized to the meaning that is available in the unplugged world. Again, it's for this reason that everything in the media world must be bigger, faster, louder, more all-encompassing, and more hyperrealistic than what it was only six months ago. No longer is it enough to sit and listen to music, we must have a video to go with it. No longer is it enough to ride a stationary bicycle, we must have a video to go with it. No longer is it enough to have dinner at the table, we must have a video to go with it. No longer is it enough to have friends over for company, we must have a video to go with it. No longer is it enough to see the sights, we must have a video to go with it. And this is just videos. Let's not forget about people who are bored in a car, a plane, a bus, a taxi, an elevator, and thus call someone or check their messages. And let's not forget about children who are bored at home, at school, in the car, at their grandparents' house, and so must be jacked in to a constant stream of passive stimulation.

Add to this a third ingredient and we arrive at the recipe for the psychological and behavioral disaster we currently face in the public sphere. As noted, the first ingredient is a steady increase in stimuli in your environments, most of which come from media technology such as televisions, radios, mobile phones and pagers, computers, CD headphones, portable technology such as PDAs and GameBoys, and strap-on technology such as wearable computers. The second ingredient is your habituation to all this stimulation, such that the unplugged world fails to grab your attention, or at least fails to keep hold of it. The third ingredient is what I would call your general need for an optimal level of stimulation.

Just as we try to maintain an optimal comfort level for such things as indoor temperature, we also have an optimal comfort level for stimulation. At one extreme, anything more than optimal is apt to feel irritating, stressful, or overwhelming. This is obviously something that depends a great deal on individuals and their overall embeddedness in hyperculture. It differs, for example, between parents and their children. It also happens to all of us in the public realm, where businesses feel the need to plug in as much visual and auditory stimulation as possible. As these examples remind us, there is a digital divide that is growing between those who are accommodating the cultural drift into hyperculture and those who go out of their way to avoid it.[3] The latter group faces a problem, however, in that anyone who takes shelter from hyperculture is apt to become only more aware of its general violence to the senses, not to mention its transformative effects on the consciousness and civility of others. For instance, some individuals avoid the new digitally driven stadium theaters because they provide what is to them an overwhelming experience.

At the other extreme, anything less than optimal will be experienced as boring, frustrating, or anxiety-producing. While this can happen to anyone—and does—it's a special problem for those who have developed a heightened need for constant sensory stimulation.

The more sensory-addicted you become, the more you find that the unplugged world doesn't go fast enough or seem interesting enough. It is here that we find households in which the television or radio blasts continuously, functioning for the sensory-addicted family as a kind of audio and visual wallpaper. Here we also find such things as road rage, computer rage, and people's general incapacity to slow down or stop, whether in a car, on a bicycle, or on foot. I think the frustration and anger people experience under these conditions is really a reflection of their overall frustration and stress in their lives, which is then triggered under conditions of suboptimal stimulation. This is epitomized by the motorist who, when frozen in traffic, is literally brought to tears by the overwhelming incongruity between the motion of the dashboard clock—tick, tick, tick—and the motionless car.

As the notion of sensory addictions suggests, your adaptation to sensory stimulation means that you're not just habituating to growing levels of stimulation, you're also engaging in new behaviors in order to satisfy your inflated need for speed. This would not be a problem except for the fact that you probably still spend a large portion of your time in the unplugged world. As the you who is wired for the rhythm and speed of the electronic world comes face-to-face with the you who inhabits the slowness of unplugged reality, the response is to try to electrify and speed up what's left of the unplugged world. In the case of children, this is often apparent when kids are forced to cope in relatively slower realms, such as the classroom or the dinner table. As I explored in *Ritalin Nation,* the American response to this has been to accommodate children by keeping them jacked in to stimulation throughout the day, which is done through the use of stimulant drugs such as Ritalin. Another, all-too-popular solution is simply to plug in more stimulating activities at school and home. Of course, in both these instances it's obvious that we are simply accommodating our children to a distracted way of life, rather than trying to reduce their distraction by, if you will, unplugging them.

Meanwhile, in the adult world you find that, as you move back and forth between the accelerated and the slow, relationships become more stressed. There is, on the one hand, the social self, who moves at a relatively slow and constant speed determined by the pace and realities of real relationships with real people. The psychological development of relationships between parents and their children, between friends, and between lovers takes place within a temporal space that cannot be sped up. When it is, the ground upon which relationships are built becomes unstable, undermining the essential fabric that binds all enduring connections and feeds the self's inner, human needs. There is, on the other hand, the hurried, digital self, who moves at an increasingly faster pace and who spends increasing amounts of time jacked in to what is or will soon be a fully digital hyperworld. The fact that we are accommodating ourselves to a distracted way of life thus means that we as a society will be seeing a greater fraying of all meaningful relationships, accompanied no doubt by the rise of a fully wired digital self that is "connected" all the time. An advertisement for Blackberry wireless devices tells all:

Blackberry is wireless email made incredibly easy. It's the best way to stay connected and manage your inbox while on the go. No dialing-in. No antenna to raise. No effort required. . . . "I've been using Blackberry for the past two months and have found it to be a transforming experience. . . . Always connected, always on, and always there."[4]

PHARMACOLOGICAL AID

on our way to digitopia, drugs have become

prosthetics for a self under siege

Psychotropic drugs and digital media may appear to have nothing in common, but in fact both are powerful technologies taken up in the aid of the postmodern self. They are both prosthetic technologies, in other words, which help you cope in a world tailored not to your social and psychological needs but to society's contrived economic and hyperindividualistic priorities. By this I do not mean that psychotropic drugs and media technology are only or necessarily prosthetic technologies. I simply mean that a very significant portion of their use today falls within this realm.

As suggested by the drama of the digital self, millions of Americans have fallen out of balance with the one realm of experience that can bring the psychological self a true sense of well-being: the social realm. Running (and Web surfing) back and forth among the work realm, the consumer realm, the virtual realm, and the social realm, you're at home nowhere. The symptoms of living such a life naturally vary in form and intensity across individuals, sexes, races, and groups and include everything from psychosomatic problems to personality disorders to behavioral problems with hyperactivity and aggression to debilitating problems of anxiety and depression. Despite the fact that not all of us are affected equally, there can be no doubt that, for a long time now, the self has taken refuge from an alienating world by using both drugs and media technology as quick-fix solutions.

In the digital age, as the gap continues to grow between the reality provided by the unplugged versus the plugged-in world, we are led to wonder: Will we permit advances in biomedical and cybernetic technology simply to continue to provide more powerful prosthetics for a society that will, as a result, be rendered all the more toxic? Or will an understanding of this vicious cycle emerge in the public consciousness, such that we will come to realize that all this entertainment and medicine is really just an illusion—one that conceals the hole in our culture down which so much humanity is now being flushed?

When looking at the rise of Prozac-like drugs in the last decade or so, it's clear that we live in a time when our understanding of everything psychological has been turned upside down.[1] People diagnosed with cancer make radical changes in how they live, believing that the mind-body connection could make the difference between life and death. Meanwhile, people suffering from psychological distress— malaise, depression, anxiety, angst—leave the structure of their lives basically untouched, turning to medicine instead. If there's a death in the family, people don't go to their priest, minister, or rabbi; they go to their doctor. Biology is the new God, and drugs such as Prozac are becoming the spiritual leaders of our time.

To help in our understanding of the origins of this biomedical revolution and how it dovetails with people's general escape into a digital tomorrow, this essay examines what might be called the "Prozac revolution." Here I am singling out Prozac not as a special drug but rather as a drug that has become iconic for our time, representing as it does the overall explosion of psychotropic drug use in the 1980s and '90s. This trend toward expanding psychiatric diagnostic categories, such that they now subsume huge segments of the American population, began long before the Prozac revolution. What made the

Prozac revolution an actual revolution was something else, namely, the social philosophy that was packaged along with it. Peter Kramer, in his bestselling book *Listening to Prozac,* calls this philosophy *cosmetic psychopharmacology.* This refers to the idea that new designer drugs are now being synthesized that are uniquely tailored to fit our psychological needs—not to make us well but to make us, in the words of Peter Kramer, "better than well." This drug ideology couples perfectly with the ideology of the digital age: both tap into the same utopian technological spirit in American society, and both function as technologies of the self that accommodate individuals to a dying and dysfunctional social realm.

Let us look at the specifics of the Prozac revolution more closely, if only to reveal its profound ideological significance (and scientific insignificance) for the digital self. From 1980 to 1989, in the widening context of our culture of discontent, the Prozac revolution was born. During these years the number of prescriptions filled for antidepressants in the United States more than doubled. In 1987 alone, 11 million people worldwide were taking Prozac, half of them in the United States. These drugs also became popular for America's youth.[2] In 1992, between 4 million and 6 million prescriptions for Prozac were filled for American children and adolescents, and this number continued to increase exponentially throughout the 1990s (in fact, both antidepressant and stimulant drugs are being used increasingly with infants and toddlers). In 1999, Prozac was the number three–selling drug, with more than 76 million prescriptions filled.[3] Today, there are roughly 28 million users of antidepressants in America—almost 1 in 10 Americans.

To many these numbers signify medical progress and greater public awareness of so-called mental diseases. What they actually signify is the continual narrowing down of our conceptions of humanity and selfhood, where all that is psychological and social is being rewritten as biological.[4] As a result, the psychological distress that characterizes life in the middle years is now commonly viewed as a mere "symptom," "sign," or "manifestation" of some inner illness or disease—and millions of Americans have now been duped into believing they suffer from a chemical imbalance in the brain. In short, the psychological has been redefined as biological and then treated as medical.

Denial about the meaning of the Prozac revolution runs deep in our culture. Hailed as the product of recent breakthroughs in the sciences of psychopathology, pharmacology, and neuroscience, Prozac and other "new" antidepressant drugs were presented to the depressed and anxious public as enlightened tools of "cutting-edge" medical science. In 1994, *Newsweek* printed on its cover, "Shy? Forgetful? Anxious? Fearful? Obsessed? . . . Science will let you change your personality with a pill."[5] The "enlightened" National Public Radio reported much the same: "A greater understanding of the brain and chemistry has given psychotherapists a whole new battery of chemical weapons—drugs like Prozac, Xanax, Paxil, and Risperidone—against a host of mental illnesses, including depression, schizophrenia, and anxiety. . . . Breakthroughs in psychopharmacology, the study of how drugs affect the mind, have led some doctors even to say that they can cure depression."

In truth, the so-called medical breakthroughs of the Prozac revolution never happened. Few realize, for example, that several thousand compounds were tested by Eli Lilly before Prozac was stumbled upon. Few realize also that many of the SSRIs—the selective serotonin reuptake inhibitors (which also includes Paxil and Zoloft)—were never brought to market because they were not at all effective in treating problems of depression (Eli Lilly was not even the first drug company to develop an SSRI).[6] Furthermore, the oft-cited claim that Prozac and the other SSRIs were designed with a new understanding of what causes depression is false. The story often heard with respect to this claim is that earlier antidepressants, the tricyclics, acted on two neurotransmitter systems in the brain— serotonin and norepinephrine—only one of which was causally connected to depression. According to this story, researchers concluded that a drug that acted only on serotonin would be more clinically effective and, at the same time, have fewer side effects than drugs acting on both serotonin and norepinephrine. Hence the development of the SSRIs, which work by acting only on serotonin. Peter Kramer writes in *Listening to Prozac:* "Imipramine is 'dirty' in its main effects and its side effects because it affects both norepinephrine and serotonin. Once Imipramine's mechanism of action was understood, pharmacologists set out to synthesize a 'clean' antidepressant—one as effective as Imipramine but more specific in its action." With this understanding in place, Eli Lilly claims in its ads in popular magazines: "To help bring serotonin levels closer to normal, the medicine doctors now prescribe most often is Prozac."

This claim of SSRIs as magic bullets is myth, pure and simple. A close examination of two popular magazine articles, one in *Time* and the other in *Newsweek,* makes this clear:

In 1994, *Newsweek* declared that the mysteries of the brain had been unlocked, leading to huge medical advances: "Now the same scientific insights into the brain that led to the development of Prozac are raising the prospect of nothing less than made-to-order personalities.... Research that once mapped the frontiers of disease—identifying the brain chemistry involved in depression, paranoia and schizophrenia—is today closing in on the chemistry of normal personality."[7]

However, three years later, *Time* suggested that these aspects of the brain are at best poorly understood: "For depression, bulimia, obesity and the rest of the serotonin-related disorders, however, no one knows for sure what part of the brain is involved or exactly why the drugs work.... The entire history of serotonin and of drugs that affect it has been largely a process of trial and error marked by chance discoveries, surprise connections and unanticipated therapeutic effects.... The tools used to manipulate serotonin in the brain are more like pharmacological machetes than they are like scalpels."[8]

Still, the 1997 article in *Time* did manage to promote the myth that a better understanding of the brain has led to new SSRI antidepressants: "In the 1960s, a second class of antidepressants emerged.... [They] had major side effects, though, including profound drowsiness and heart palpitations. The reason, scientists generally agreed, was that they affected brain chemistry too broadly. The research seemed to point to serotonin as the most important mood-enhancing chemical, though not the only one, and so neurochemists set about looking for a drug that would boost the influence of serotonin alone. In 1974, after a decade of work, Eli Lilly came up with Prozac, first of the so-called selective serotonin reuptake inhibitors, or SSRIs, and it was finally approved by the FDA in 1987."

This claim becomes suspect, however, once we know that the very latest antidepressants are said to act only on norepinephrine, the very neurotransmitter suggested by *Time* and Peter Kramer as doing nothing for depression while causing the preponderance of side effects. As the *Time* article noted, "Psychiatrists in Europe are buzzing about a new drug, reboxetine, that has just been approved for use in Britain and seems to be even more effective than Prozac for severely depressed patients. Marketed under the brand name Edronax, it totally ignores serotonin and targets another brain chemical, norepinephrine, which is also known to have a powerful effect on mood."

How could both these statements occur in the same article? They could because the *Time* article avoids mentioning that it was in fact norepinephrine that had been originally identified as unrelated to depression, stating only that "The research seemed to point to serotonin as the most important mood-enhancing chemical."

Finally, the *Newsweek* article brings us full circle when telling us that the more recent drug Effexor works more effectively than the SSRIs by acting on both norepinephrine and serotonin: "Effexor . . . enhances both serotonin and norepinephrine, a second chemical messenger affecting mood. With its broader effect, Effexor should help some depressed patients who don't respond to Prozac."

These passages indicate that most Americans probably have little understanding of what they are really doing when they participate in the Prozac revolution. How could they, since even the media and their quoted "experts" cannot tell a coherent story. What we do know for sure is that people do not suffer from chemical imbalances in the brain. Drugs such as Prozac act on serotonin levels almost immediately, yet their clinical effects take days or even several weeks to manifest themselves, if they do so at all.

We also know that Prozac and its ilk are not new, more effective compounds that somehow correct these imbalances. That is, research has now demonstrated that the SSRIs are in fact no more effective in treating problems of depression than were the tricyclic compounds—and may have even more serious side effects.[9] Finally, we know that these problems cannot be explained in strictly biological terms since those cannot explain why, as noted earlier, these problems are on the rise.[10]

These passages should also make it clear that the Prozac revolution was not a revolution in pharmacological or brain science. Again, the Prozac age, like the digital age, represents a revolution in social philosophy. The collective ethos envelops both cosmetic psychopharmacology and the digital information age, a single, totalizing framework in which you are taught to seek out technology- and consumer-based solutions to what are not in the last instance individual problems. What Paul Goodman has said about technology generally seems especially appropriate here: "Whether or not it draws on new scientific research, technology is a branch of moral philosophy, not of science."[11] Thus, whatever the psychological symptoms, we have to consider the possibility that the vast majority of them are ultimately structural problems held in place by a number of institutional forces, all of which have to do with the three roles identified earlier: worker, consumer, and patient.

In the future, the link between psychotropic drugs and digital media as powerful technologies of the self will become increasingly obvious, as more lifestyle drugs are brought to market to help you cope in the middle years of the digital age. In addition to cosmetic psychopharmacology, the larger category of lifestyle drugs includes everything from drugs used for sexual dysfunction and sexual desire to drugs used for hair loss, wrinkles, appetite, weight loss, and more. All these drugs are lifestyle drugs in that each plays a part in the overall move toward a cybernetic culture. As we have seen, this is a culture in which the boundary between the biological self and the technological other is rapidly disappearing.

Julian Stallabrass, writing in the *New Left Review,* summarizes the situation as we look to the future of the digital age:

> The real world is in perhaps terminal decline, and threatens to bury its inhabitants in obsolete consumer goods, an ever rising tide of trash. People turn their backs on reality, into drugs, into cyberspace, or, for the less active, into an enveloping form of television which imparts the sensory experiences of its stars. Cyberspace is at once an ideological inverse image of this world, and what helps to maintain the power of those who govern it. Nevertheless, for those who regularly inhabit it, even the real world comes to seem like cyberspace, as the virtual takes on a reality which often has material effects, and the material acquires an unreal virtuality. Given this scenario, the question arises, why does anyone want to develop dystopia? Among the reasons which immediately spring to mind are its supposed technical inevitability coupled with dissatisfaction with currently fixed identities and activities, and also that there might be a career in it.[12]

This about sums it up: The road to digitopia is paved with a cynicism of technological inevitability, a dissatisfaction with one's inner and outer life, and the need for a well-paying job.

PART IV

THE
GEOGRAPHY
OF
DIGITOPIA

We're lost but we're making good time.

Yogi Berra

LIVING IN TIMELESS TIME

AND PLACELESS SPACE

in search of place in the age of cyberspace

If digitopia is where we're headed, place is the last thing we'll find. In this essay, I explain why.

Earlier I suggested that building a digital alternative to material reality should not be dismissed out of hand, as such a world could be programmed with virtues far surpassing those of the unplugged world of today. While I have not changed my mind, I want to clarify this conclusion by describing what it takes to create *place*—real place—and why, en route to digitopia, we are not apt to find it. The implication of this is not that the pursuit of digitopia is a doomed enterprise. To the contrary, it's exactly because a fully wired (and wireless) world is not apt to satisfy our growing, if misdiagnosed, yearnings for place that our pursuit of an all-encompassing digital matrix is sure to continue.

Let me clarify what I mean by "place" by identifying three of its key attributes. The immediate impulse is to suggest that place is represented first and foremost by physical space. This is not correct. Its most central attribute can be defined instead as *persistence,* without which place does not exist. Persistence is ultimately a way of making meaning, meaning that comes about over time through the self's connectedness with an enduring social and ecological realm.

The German philosopher Martin Heidegger was perhaps the most profound thinker to address this issue, which he defined in terms of "being-in-the-world."[1] For Heidegger, the notion of persistence existed as a kind of "dwelling" in the world, where you're enriched through a deep connectedness to your surroundings. The idea here is to reach beyond the surface of reality to tap into the more meaningful world that lies beneath. For Heidegger, this connectedness is also like the worn social fabric I have been discussing, which over time becomes so familiar as a source of meaning that it's no longer noticed. It is most likely to be noticed when it falls off, which is why the subject of *meaning* is such an active area of scholarship in the humanities and social sciences.[2] For today we "dwell" less and less in shared everyday activities that give rise to enduring structures of meaning. The nomadic self of today is more akin to a water-skier who, in picking up speed, rises to the surface, skimming across the water while hardly getting wet.

Place represents, in other words, a kind of coming together of the continuity of time and enduring materiality of space, which fuse together to create a sense of permanence and stability. While persistence is usually associated with a fixed physical environment, such as a village or neighborhood, it's not necessarily so. For example, hunters and gatherers probably experienced a real sense of place, but this place was constituted more in the shared experience of the members of the group; place was shared more in the persistence of rituals among familiar individuals than in the persistence of some local environment.

A second critical attribute of place might be defined in terms of *gravity.* This exists when your life is endowed with a sense of belonging that comes from being weighed down by shared responsibility. This can be found in relationships, as in the example of marriage, or in family, as in the example of carrying on a family business, or in the larger community, as in the example of shared governance. In any case, gravity represents the interlocking dependencies that tie us together, which then create a sense of being at home in the world.

The existentialist novelist Milan Kundera gives us a near-perfect example in *The Unbearable Lightness of Being.* As the title suggests, Kundera wants us to reconsider whether an unbounded individual—an individual who is free to do whatever he or she wishes to do—should really be held up as the greatest possible individual or societal achievement. Kundera's Tomas, the central figure of the story, struggles to maintain his prized, selfish independence, eventually acknowledging to himself how much more he gains through what becomes a truly mutual and shared relationship with Anna. For Kundera, this is not about giving oneself wholly over to another (which is not what Tomas does in any case). As is suggested by the drama of the evolving self, the question is really one of balance: too much gravity crushes the individual spirit; too little creates a lightness that is, if not unbearable, at least existentially vapid. Ultimately, without some gravity pushing down on one's life, the relationships that hold place together become untenable and break apart. What Kundera's novel shows, I think, is how difficult it is to bring such relationships into being in the absence of an organic source of gravity in one's life, for at this point gravity becomes something that is avoided rather than pursued.

One obvious realm where place still exists in America today is among the Old Order Amish. However attractive or unattractive one finds Amish life, it nevertheless provides a relatively fixed point of reference from which we can gauge our own loss of place. Despite what is generally believed, the Amish have not demonized technology, although they do attempt to understand and control its transformative effects on their everyday life and consciousness. For example, houses are not furnished with telephones, but there are community phones, which are kept at some distance from the home. This way the phone does not become so ubiquitous in their lives that, by bringing those who are far away so close, it has the unintended effect of creating distance between those at home and those in the immediate community. A comparable example was described in *The Economist:* "Yet the Internet can clash with the monks' way of life: instead of retreating from the world, they can hook up with it by going online. So Father Francis, Mepkin's abbot . . . , keeps a tight rein on Internet use; only a handful of monks have access to it."[3] Instead of excluding the telephone (or the Internet), the Amish (and the monks) have mastered it in such a way that it serves their way of life, rather than vice versa.

Through such mediation, the Amish have been largely successful in avoiding technological temptation, just as they have been successful in maintaining what is called a *high-context culture,* which is a third identifiable attribute of place. "High context" means that everyday life remains contextualized within the material world. The noted scholar of Amish culture John Hostetler describes this in his book *Amish Society,* noting how mainstream America has gradually become a low-context culture by comparison, with people's sense of reality becoming disconnected from direct or firsthand experience in the here and now. In a low-context culture, experience derives less from direct relationships with one another and what is left of the natural world, and more from abstracted relationships mediated by a technology of mass media. Hostetler writes:

> The flow of information into the Amish community is highly selective. Furthermore, the Amish are keenly aware of their own screening process. Direct exposure to mass communication systems is greatly reduced. This screening protects members, and their nervous systems, from information overload. What the Amish pay attention to . . . and what they ignore are different from the choices of low-contexting cultures. Information overload is handled differently in the two cultures. Most Americans are exposed to large amounts of information daily and are scarcely aware of a screening process between themselves and the outside world.

Amish society is an extreme example, to be sure, but it illustrates the three overlapping facets of place I have identified: persistence, gravity, and context. We come across the Amish and are in awe of the lives they live, which I think is another sign of our yearning for place. However, we also know that a life of such sacrifices would not be possible for us. In fact, despite our yearnings for place, ethical notions such as responsibility, commitment, and persistence appear to many in these wireless times as antiquated notions that are downright antithetical to living "the good life." If the digital information age represents one thing above all others, it's not place or permanence but their opposite: *mobility.*

Danny Hillis, a supercomputer designer, writes, "Rituals, once our most powerful device for restraining the passage of time, seem to have lost their potency. In the time of my childhood, Monday was wash day, Tuesday was market day, and Sunday was worship and a day for rest. In this age of 24-hour-a-day, seven-days-a-week convenience, I have begun to lose my bearings. I fly from time zone to time zone, living in CNN time, out of touch even with the rhythms of my own flesh."[4] Of course, this is all the more possible in the digital age. A magazine advertisement from Toshiba Electronics: "Cruise the halls of freedom with abandon. You now have the license to do what you want, where you want, and when you want. . . . Come and go with a newfound freedom that fits neatly within your hands. . . . It's technology that sets you free." Print advertisements from Lucent Technologies tell us: "Sarah's work takes her everywhere the wind blows. She works for an aeroelectric power company, and work is rarely at the office. But now she can do business anywhere. . . . Everything from interactive games with 3D graphics to online banking to video e-mail is always at your fingertips. When you change the way people communicate, you change the way they live. Lucent Technologies. We make the Internet mobile."

Mobility of this kind is inherently antagonistic to place because it substitutes an unbounded and fleeting virtuality for a bounded and enduring reality.[5] Persistence over time is replaced with persistent change; the pressure of gravity is replaced with the pressure to take flight; and the truth and identity of a contextualized life are replaced by the relativism and multiple identities of a decontextualized existence. Julian Stallabrass makes the point as regards the Internet:

The greatest freedom cyberspace promises is that of recasting the self: from static beings, bound by the body and betrayed by appearances, Net surfers may reconstruct themselves in a multiplicity of dazzling roles, changing from moment to moment according to whim. From being restricted to single time and place, the Net being may distribute itself over the wired-up globe and make its acts and statements eternal.[6]

Without an enduring social fabric in which to wrap ourselves, we live less an intentional and embedded existence and more an impulsive and frenetic one. As suggested earlier, the lifestyle approach to finding meaning in everyday life has been the result, with us forfeiting a quality of life for a mere quantity of it. In the digital information age, an infinite depth of experience in the material world—place— becomes an infinite surface of experience spread out over timeless time and placeless space: cyberspace.

As this suggests, with the growing absence of place in people's lives, we as a society are experiencing a transformation in the basic dimensions of time and space. Timeless time and placeless space refer to the fact that, in the global, digital information age, time and space are losing their bounded structure.[7] Like the transformations of consciousness produced by changes in media technologies, transformations of time and space are not new. In medieval times and before, people lived in highly circumscribed spaces, and their sense of time had a circular or seasonal structure. As the world went modern, people began to travel greater distances and to lose their sense of a shared identity carried from one generation to the next. The result was that their sense of space collapsed, just as did circular time: the world became smaller, and time was flattened out into a linear structure of past (I'm born), present (I live), and future (I die). In the postmodern era, a third transformation is taking place: linear time is being absorbed into an ever-expanding now—a timeless time—and collapsed space is being further collapsed into placeless space. As Rosabeth Moss Kanter has described it, "In the digital age, time becomes increasingly nonlinear.

The past is the present. All times can coexist; time lags between action and reaction diminish, gaps between places close."[8]

Together these two dimensionless dimensions form a new hyper-cosmology characterized by an infinite inner space: no longer are we moving toward an expanded reality that incorporates a larger universe, perhaps even one that includes sentient beings from beyond planet Earth. Instead, the utopia of digitopia is a collapsed reality that incorporates nothing more than an immortal self digitized and then downloaded into a virtual machine. On the way to digitopia, instead of looking outward to shimmering skies, we find ourselves staring into glowing screens. What matters today is not an ancient stream of light that reveals our sacred past, but a perpetually newborn flood of light that distracts us from our empty present.[9]

With mobility as the modus operandi, you are no longer a citizen of place; you become a nomad of infinite inner space.

CONSTRUCTING DIGITOPIA

making our digital dreamworld

a technological reality

At this point readers are probably wondering about the possibilities of humankind being downloaded into a virtual machine. And many are likely to doubt it. If the reason is not existential or ethical, it's technological: digitopia—a digital matrix that provides infinite escape and immortality—cannot be built because of an insuperable chasm that exists between human consciousness, on the one hand, and machine programming, on the other (i.e., the ontological gulf). As correct as this may sound, it deserves a closer look.

In Part I we looked at the codification of the material world that digital technology allows. There I suggested that this technology provides a basic means to turn all that exists in nature and society into information—information that, when coupled with other technologies, could be used to reinvent them. One example is the digital technology used for research in biotechnology, which includes the sequencing and storage of the genomes of different species of plants and animals, humans included, that can then be compared and contrasted, reorganized, and reinserted back into nature. If nature is the sum of its parts and we can get to the bottom of these parts and codify them as information, it's a logical conclusion that, when turning to the task of making the parts whole again, we are likely to build—or attempt to build—something more to our liking (or at least to the liking of those who profit from such manipulations).

In the area of genetically modified (GM) foods, this is already taking place. Specific genes from one species of animal or plant are being inserted into the cells of other species of animals or plants, producing self-replicating hybrids that are said to yield larger crops and be, for a time at least, more resistant to predators and infection. In the United States, the USDA has approved more than fifty GM crops, and about half of all the world's soybean and corn production contains genes taken from other plant species. The long-term ecological consequences of these manipulations have not always been anticipated, nor could they be. In one now-familiar case, researchers found that when the larvae of monarch butterflies fed on the pollen of GM corn, it limited their capacity to reproduce.[1]

Another example is nanotechnology, which does much the same for the physical world, creating self-propelled structures that can even cross over into living systems to affect biological processes.[2] In the world of nanotechnology, the universe of the nanometer, where things are measured in billionths of a meter, becomes our playground. Nanotechnology necessarily forces us down to this size because it seeks to take hold of atomic particles (and the molecules they create) and build a new world from the ground up. For example, while each of the millions of microscopic transistor switches on a Pentium processor consists of about 1 billion atoms, nanotechnologists and others are pursuing quantum computing, where each transistor consists of nothing more than a single atom.

If nanoscience sounds to you like Tinkertoys for grown-ups, you're right, although students of nanomechanics have much more exotic plans in mind. Nature builds a lot of impressively small things, such as proteins, viruses, and living cells, and the nanotechnologists of today have high hopes of engineering synthetic versions of these same building blocks of life, creating—in God-like fashion—something out of nothing. Ray Kurzweil, a self-proclaimed prophet of the digital age (and author of *The Age of Spiritual Machines*), believes, for example, that "Nanobot technology will provide fully immersive, totally convincing virtual reality," which he envisions happening when nanorobots invade the brain to simulate a completely virtual experience in orchestral fashion.[3]

That nanotechnology can "turn man into machine" is something we are already experiencing. By this I do not mean that we are already equipped to build complex organisms, atom by atom, molecule by molecule, protein by protein. I mean that the advocates of nanotechnology are already in the process of redefining humans *as* machines, with no special equipment required. This is occurring gradually and imperceptibly as journalists and others "educate" (i.e., hype) the public about the ideas of nanotechnology. "Every cell is a living example of nanotechnology," writes Michael D. Lemonick in *Time* magazine in June 2000, "not only does it convert fuel into energy, but it also fabricates and pumps out proteins and enzymes according to the software encoded in its dna [*sic*]. By recombining dna from different species, genetic engineers have already learned to build new nanodevices—bacterial cells, for example, that pump out medically useful human hormones."[4]

Notice how in this example the writer translates biological processes shaped over millions of years of evolution into mechanical processes that can be harnessed to serve a momentary whim. Having done this, he goes on to suggest that if nature can be so adjusted, why not simply make it anew? "But biotechnology is limited by the tasks cells already know how to carry out. Nanotech visionaries have much more ambitious notions. Imagine a nanomachine that could take raw carbon and arrange it, atom by atom, into a perfect diamond. . . . Or a device that cruises the human bloodstream, seeks out cholesterol deposits on vessel walls and disassembles them." (Mr. Lemonick appears not to realize that constructing diamonds with ease would make them banal and worthless, and that removing cholesterol deposits with ease would probably only encourage obesity.)

A similar example, drawing the same conclusion, is found in an essay in *The Sciences* in 2000: "The idea of placing millions of autonomous nanorobots inside one's body might seem odd, even alarming. But the fact is that the body already teems with a vast number of mobile nanodevices, built not by human hands but by nature. . . . If nanorobotics becomes a reality, it will not stop at eliminating disease; it will actually improve on the gifts of nature."[5] It is by being presented with "harmless" examples such as these that the general public comes to view the biological building blocks of organisms as just interchangeable parts of a larger machine, with the road paved to that future time when such descriptions will become a reality.

Still, this is only the conceptual stage, and it's a far cry from taking the next big step, which is literally to connect mind and machine. As biotechnology and nanotechnology continue on their march toward the digital future, two other areas of technology are also keeping pace, both of which will play their own critical role in the building of digitopia. The first of these is artificial intelligence (AI); the second is neuroscience. These two areas represent the two sides of the interface between mind and machine.

When considering AI, we tend to underestimate its potential to simulate intelligence and life. One reason is that we as a society have a long-standing tendency to narrow our definition of being human each time AI expands. When machines began to do complex computing, computing was no longer deemed central to being human. When machines began to assemble objects, the skills required for assembly were no longer deemed central to being human. When machines began to perceive human language and speech, such perceptions were no longer deemed central to being human. When machines began to engage in advanced tactics and strategies (as in games such as chess), such cognitive skills were no longer deemed central to being human.

A second reason people underestimate AI is that they assume its rate of progress will continue to be as slow as it has been thus far. As was stressed for media technology, the pace of technological change has been accelerating throughout history, which is why new technologies are emerging today at an unprecedented speed. In its short history, beginning in the 1950s, AI has generally failed to live up to the expectations raised in the public sphere. The considerable advances being made in digital computing will not by themselves solve this problem, however, because the problem has less to do with computing and more to do with conceptual and philosophical confusions about the nature of mind and consciousness. By assuming that intelligence is something built into the brain, AI engineers have persisted in trying to reverse-engineer intelligence, with the human brain as their guide. That is, they have tried to build smart machines. This mired AI down for decades, but things are now changing.

AI engineers have finally caught on to the idea that they do not need to build smart machines, only machines that are capable of *becoming* smart (i.e., machines that can learn). One AI researcher, Igor Aleksander, writes, "This concern distinguishes between a machine which relies on its experience and one which is programmed in great detail to perform logical operations. The latter could never be sufficiently complete to qualify in a search for artificial intelligence. . . . The domain of [artificial] neural networks has come to the fore because it does not require detailed planning by a programmer or design by a designer. Learning is the primary property of neural systems."[6] This shift in paradigm comes from a general change of perspective in various disciplines, stimulated by neuroscientific research showing that the neural wiring of complex nervous systems is nothing like that of the circuitry used in digital computing. Before going into this further, let me just make the point: given the recent change in the dominant paradigm in AI, we can no longer assume that AI and related areas will continue to develop at a snail's pace. AI engineers are now busy building learning machines, and these machines—in combination with current computing speeds—will soon begin to advance by leaps and bounds.

To illustrate this idea of a deductive, learning machine, let me give a crude example. Say we want to create a device that understands a spoken language. The first problem is to make sure the device can distinguish the words of the language, which it must do in order to convert them into digital code. To do this we could perhaps program all the words (or sounds) the language contains, but we could also build the computer simply to learn what they are from experience. This would have a variety of advantages, not least of which is the fact that the machine would learn whatever language it was exposed to, and from whatever people and dialect to which it was exposed. How could this be done? It's not as difficult as it sounds.

As long as the computer can analyze the structure of sounds that make up words, it can be programmed to parse these sounds into words, assuming it's given enough instances of the language to do so (note that, depending on social class, a child hears somewhere between 10 million and 30 million words within the first three years of life, albeit some words much more than others).[7] To give an example, consider the phrases "the-red-bicycle" and "a-red-truck." These two sound strings both contain the sound "red" surrounded by other sounds; that is, "red" is a common denominator of the two phrases. After comparing them and others, the computer would tag "red" as a possible word, waiting to see if more instances show up before determining that it is, according to some programmed criteria. In the meantime, the device would also hear sounds that include "red" but are not the word "red," such as "redness" and "Alfred." The device could identify these words as well. If "ness" is never detected except with certain other sounds (such as "red," "well," "mad," "quick"), the computer would assign "ness" to those words, rather than identifying two words (e.g., "madness" versus "mad" and "ness"). The task of detecting that "Alfred" is not two words is more difficult, but it too would be a common denominator in the language (e.g., "if-Alfred-arrives" versus "when-Alfred-stops"). Taken as a whole, this identification process could give rise to the learning of the words of the language in much the same way as occurs in the real nervous systems of humans (and animals, to boot; after all, doesn't your dog know its own name?).

Of course, this is a hypothetical example, and it's meant only to illustrate the idea that a learning machine is much more powerful when given the basic capacity to learn, rather than given what it is we actually want it to know. An analogy is evolution by natural selection, in which a process of selecting heritable traits has led to vast complexity and variation in species (and their traits and capacities) over hundreds of millions of years. Note as well that this example does not consist of the machine learning the meanings of the words. To endow a machine with semantic capacity is much more difficult. The device would need a massive capacity to process and store experience, and it would need some other sensors that would facilitate this gaining of experience. Consider, for example, how a child learns the actual meaning of words.

Naturally, a child learns what it means to have a bicycle by riding one. But the child also learns what the sound "bicycle" means by having it paired with an image of a bicycle, a toy bicycle, or a real bicycle. One thing that humans do easily but that all other animals do poorly, if at all, is learn these kinds of meaningful relationships in leapfrog fashion.[8] For example, if a child is explicitly taught the relationship between b-i-c-y-c-l-e (A) and a picture of a bicycle (B), and is also explicitly taught the relationship between b-i-c-y-c-l-e (A) and the sound "bicycle" (C), he or she will learn the transitive relationship without any explicit teaching—i.e., a picture of a bicycle (B) goes with the sound "bicycle" (C). The teaching of the first two gives rise to the third. Again,

> teach the first relationship:
>   b-i-c-y-c-l-e and a picture of a bicycle,
> then teach the second relationship:
>   b-i-c-y-c-l-e and the sound "bicycle,"
> and the transitive relationship will emerge:
>   the sound "bicycle" goes with the picture of a bicycle.

As psychological research in this area has now demonstrated, this emergent process of learning produces an explosion of new behaviors. In the above example, two relationships were taught (A→B and A→C). From this, four new relationships emerge: the symmetrical relationships (B→A and C→A) and the transitive relationships

(B→C and C→B). If a total of three relationships is taught, nine new relationships emerge, including six transitive relationships (teaching A→B, A→C, and A→D gives rise to B→A, C→A, D→A, B→C, C→B, B→D, D→B, C→D, and D→C)—and this continues to expand exponentially with each added factor. What is the implication of this? It is that with a limited amount of experience, the human brain spontaneously gives rise to a considerable amount of new functional bchaviors appropriate to the prevailing environment (e.g., a child tells us that the picture of a bicycle goes with the sound "bicycle" even though she has never been taught to do so).

Not all of these emergent responses will be correct in the real world, since categories overlap and are contextually framed. To give the simplest example, when the instruction "different" or "opposite" is given to children in a choice task, the picture of a bicycle no longer goes with the sound "bicycle" (instead, a picture of a lamp or comb might be chosen). What is the implication of this? It is that even if many of these emergent relations are inappropriate in a variety of contexts (or even all contexts), this kind of emergent learning in humans gives rise to an explosion of variation in behavior. We know from the evolution of species via natural selection that variation is a necessary ingredient in creating complex outcomes (in the present case, the outcome is complex behavior).[9] Over time, some of this novel behavior will be selccted by the environment in certain contexts, while other behaviors will not.[10] Without such variation in behavior in the first place, however, most complex learning by humans, human language included, would not occur.[11]

Still, you ask, what is the main implication of all this learning for the project of connecting mind and machine? Well, it tells us that there is something unique about the neural networks of the human brain that gives rise to emergent behaviors. As this unique capacity comes to be understood, there is every indication that it could be reproduced in artificial systems. One reason why is that this capacity appears to be a very general one that does not involve highly specific neurophysiological structures in the human brain. Instead, it appears to result from the neural density of brain cells and the vast array of neural networks in the human brain (in other words, the differences between human and other primate learning are a function more of quantitative differences than of qualitative ones—a view that is supported by the considerable genetic similarities between humans and some other primates). The British neuroscientist Susan Greenfield draws much the same conclusion with regard to consciousness:

> Consciousness is spatially multiple, yet effectively single at any one time. It is an emergent property of non-specialized groups of neurons that are continuously variable with respect to an epicentre. . . . If enough neurons are recruited, consciousness will ensue for that moment. In my view, therefore, the critical factor is not qualitative; it is much more sensible to think in terms of quantity of neurons engaged.[12]

As the analogy to natural selection suggests, the process that gives rise to complexity in behavior, which in turn gives rise to our sense of intelligence, personality, and so on, operates according to a simple but powerful system of variation, selection, and retention. In the sphere of natural selection, this refers to variation in heritable phenotypes (i.e., traits that are expressed), selection of some phenotypes by the environment, and a retention of these phenotypes over time through the preservation of the underlying genotypes (i.e., DNA sequences, or genes). In the psychological sphere of behavioral selection, this refers to variation in behavioral phenotypes (during one's lifetime), selection of some of these phenotypes by the environment, and a retention of them over time through the preservation of the genotypes (i.e., specific neural connections in the brain).[13] Being intelligent has a lot to do with learning in an intelligent environment, and thus behavioral and neuroscience researchers are reminding AI engineers that learning systems can acquire great complexity even though their underlying "programs" may be relatively simple.

The net result is this: AI engineers will indeed be able to create learning machines that mirror human capacities, and they will do so by engineering systems that mirror the degree of neural density and neural networking found in the human brain. This requires programming a machine so that, when guided by experience in a dynamic ecological world, it will construct its own "neural networks." This will require vast amounts of computing power and memory, which brings us to another obstacle in connecting mind and machine: overcoming the limits to computing power that are inherent in current silicon-chip technology. Before turning to this, let me first conclude this overview of neuroscience.

It turns out that programming computational systems that simulate neural networks is not the only advance being made in neuroscience that relates to the prospect of bridging mind and machine. There are many other important advances being made, some of which utilize brain-imaging technologies, including CAT scans, EEGs, MRIs, functional MRIs, and PET scans.[14] This is, of course, a complex and rapidly changing area, one that, as I have written elsewhere, is mired in its own conceptual confusions.[15] Nevertheless, I anticipate that these confusions will soon be overcome and researchers will begin to use imaging technologies to learn more about how brain and experience combine to produce higher-order phenomena, including "intelligence," "thought," "personality," "mind," and "self."

In terms of building an all-encompassing virtual machine, imaging technology will play a critical role in uncovering the precise nature of the neural network systems described above, especially as scans with greater resolution are developed. Still, this is new, and exactly how the brain gives rise to such phenomena as consciousness, memory, cognition, and perception remains very much a mystery. As the science writer John Horgan has argued, it seems that the more we know about brain processes, the less we know.[16] But this will probably not continue for much longer. Thousands of researchers work in the field of neuroscience within the United States alone, and the area is well endowed with both public and private moneys. Just in the past few years, in fact, research has made clear gains in identifying how different areas of the brain work in a majority-wins collaboration to produce what Marvin Minsky aptly dubbed in 1986 "the society of mind."[17] Of course these types of findings are exactly the kind that aid AI and computer engineers in modeling human thought and behavior.

If mind can in fact be modeled, modeling a human mind will nevertheless fail to occur without significantly more computing power than is currently available. At present, we have the Pentium 4 chip, which can perform as many as 8.4 billion operations per second, on its 42 million transistors.[18] This is the product of the latest doubling in processing power that has been occurring every eighteen months or so for the past thirty-five years. This exponential increase was anticipated in 1965 by Gordon Moore, cofounder of Intel, and is now called "Moore's law." But there is a problem: these advances are the product of a process that will reach its physical limitations by about 2020. If so, this would mean an end to Moore's law at a point when silicon chips contain something like 10 billion transistors. Computers will be calculating at trillions of bytes per second, and while this sounds like quite a few, it will still not be enough to mirror the mind with a machine.

To realize why, one has to remember there are about 100 billion neurons in the human brain, each of which connects with dozens or even hundreds of other neurons. These connections are called synapses, and there are about one million billion of them in a fully developed brain. This number is more easily grasped by looking at the early development of the brain, when about 2.5 trillion synapses are made each year.[19] As this suggests, for a computer to represent the kind of layered interconnectedness that gives rise to mind and consciousness would require a lot more power than can be made available through current technology. Technologist Ray Kurzweil suggests that 20 million billion neural-type calculations per second would be required, which goes well beyond the capacities of silicon chips.[20]

Whatever the number, to avoid hitting silicon bedrock will require the development of new processing formats. None of this is news to computer engineers, of course, and various new formats are already under intense investigation. An example given above was for quantum computing, in which computer engineers are hoping to turn individual atoms into on/off transistors. The motivation for all this work is not driven by researchers and inventors who have their eyes on digitopia. Their interests are much more immediate, rooted in the fact that hitting silicon bedrock would mean the end of selling a new generation of computers and video-game consoles to the public every eighteen to twenty-four months. Realizing this, I'm sure you can imagine why Moore's law is likely to persist for some time to come.

Keeping this in mind, we can now turn to a final problem: if we can build artificial minds that can learn to engage in complex thought and behavior in an ecological context, how will (or could) this lead to downloading a human brain into a virtual machine? This is a legitimate concern, as it will no doubt be easier to create a digital mind from scratch than it will to download an existing brain into a virtual machine. In answering the question, however briefly, I want to suggest two developments that would make this likely if we stay the course to digitopia. One involves technological progress, the other psychological regress.

Even the cerebral synapses of identical twins are very different at the level of individual neural connections. This means that downloading a human brain would require a 3-D mapping of the detailed neural layering of the individual brain connections while active in a variety of environmental contexts. It would then require translating this multidimensional information into digital code, which would in turn be transferred to and then represented in a constructed model that might or might not look like a human brain. When plugged in, the duplicated brain would come to life as a derivative of a human mind, which could then interact with a virtual world, which would be necessary to keep such an artificial mind alive. Whatever its content, this virtual realm would need to use the same understanding of the brain to simulate the sensory inputs, from vision to locomotion to visceral experience. The fact that individuals who have lost limbs often feel they have a "phantom limb" is further evidence that the mind would cooperate with a simulation of this nature.[21]

With this as technological progress, let me turn, finally, to what I suggest is psychological regress. In imagining a synthetic mind that mirrors a natural mind—computer cloning, if you will—we must also consider the problem of human identity. Note, first, that much of the human brain can atrophy before we notice obvious changes in behavior and self, even in an individual who is affected by, say, Parkinson's or Alzheimer's disease. This means that not every neural connection in the brain will need to be mapped in order for the mad scientists of the future to reproduce an individual's identity. In fact, the resolution in certain areas could probably be very low. Note, second, that we have seen a growing fragmentation of human identity throughout most of the twentieth century, one that will accelerate in the digital age, with all the unembodied freedoms it provides the digital self. And, finally, my point: by the time digitopia appears on the technological horizon, there is the distinct possibility that identity will have become so fragmented that downloading the mind into a virtual machine will pose fewer problems and risks, since the self will have a less unitary and integrated consciousness to preserve. After all, when I suggest that we may one day be downloaded into a virtual machine, I do not mean that this will make us whole again. Quite the contrary.

PART V

THE FUTURE
OF THE FUTURE

We played a game we couldn't win, at the utmost.

Gus Van Sant and Dan Yosh

THE (BILL) JOYS
OF TECHNOLOGY

fearing the future that already is

In April 2000, *Wired* magazine published an essay by Sun Microsystems' cofounder and chief scientist, Bill Joy, entitled "Why the Future Doesn't Need Us."[1] Broad in its scope and provocative in its conclusions, the essay attracted considerable attention. The main argument: new technologies involving genetic engineering, robotics, and nanotechnology are emerging that threaten the future well-being, if not the very existence, of life, humanity, and the planet. They are threatening, Joy argued, because they create systems too complex to understand, predict, and control, and because they have the capacity to create forms of synthetic nature that, because they are self-replicating, could overwhelm organic nature. "The replicating and evolving processes that have been confined to the natural world are about to become realms of human endeavor," writes Joy.[2] This mirrors a view presented previously by Kevin Kelly (of *Wired* magazine) in *Out of Control: The New Biology of Machines, Social Systems, and the Economic World,* although Kelly draws a very different conclusion: "The world of the made will soon be like the world of the born: autonomous, adaptable, and creative but, consequently, out of our control. I think that's a great bargain."[3] The cover of the issue containing Joy's essay shows a torn and crumpled page from some future dictionary, presumably published by robots, with "human" defined as "of, belonging to, or typical of the extinct species *Homo sapiens* <the human race>."

Joy is no anarchist revolutionary. His views are consistent with those of many radicals who question the blind, global-capitalist pursuit of powerful technologies—especially those concerning biotechnology—but he himself remains a central figure in the developing world of digital technology. I would suggest that it's Joy and his small mutiny, and not his ideas per se, that have been the real focus of all the media attention. Not surprisingly, in most instances, media coverage has given short shrift to the issues raised.

In this essay, I want to show not only that the future Bill Joy fears is in the making, but also that in many ways it's already here. In contrast to Joy's account, which suggests an eventual break in people's control over the future (and the machines that could rebuild it in their own image), I believe this break has already taken place, with the near future spinning ever more rapidly out of control. Joy fears that emerging technologies will soon give us the power to remake the world: yet current technologies already have. Joy fears that emerging technologies could lead to biological and ecological disasters: yet present technologies are already doing just this.[4] Joy fears that the human race could be replaced by emerging technologies such as sentient robots: yet we are ourselves already at risk of becoming a kind of sentient robot. Joy fears that we will develop a dangerous dependence on networked systems of intelligence: yet we already have such a dependence. Joy fears that those dissatisfied with the technological status quo could be reengineered so that they are satisfied; in fact, millions of people are already being medicated to cope with, and thus conform to, the status quo.

As I noted earlier, Joy has it right about where we are headed, more or less, but he fails to connect the darker possibilities of the future with the shadows already looming large in the present. Joy writes, "The new Pandora's boxes of genetics, nanotechnology, and robotics are almost open, yet we seem to have hardly noticed."[5] In truth, these boxes are already wide open. Let me explain why.

The notion that emerging technologies give us the power to re-make the world is, as I have argued throughout this book, clear in the case of media technology generally, and especially digital technology. The latter is remaking the world at this very moment, from the reconstruction of the "real world" to the reconstruction of the "biological world" to the reconstruction of the "natural world." And yes, this raises the specter of social and ecological disaster, espe-cially in the case of digital technology fusing with technology for genetic sequencing. However, the notion that here stands an un-opened Pandora's box is at best naive, as should be obvious given how many species' boundaries have already been crossed in manu-facturing GM foods and other synthetic nature. In fact, Joy ac-knowledges that the development of these foods "is already very far along."[6] What he fails to acknowledge is that the threat of genetic engineering lies not in the technology per se, which is in its infancy, but in the cultural and economic logic that is driving this technology forward, which has been entrenched for some time.

With an exploding world population (which has more than dou-bled since the 1950s and which will double again in thirty or so years), and with the economic destabilization of Third World coun-tries, we find ourselves in a situation in which the genetic manipu-lation of nature is justified with pictures of starving children. Bill Gates, for example, asks, "Will 'Frankenfoods' feed the world? Biotech is not a panacea, but it does promise to transform agricul-ture in many developing countries. If that promise is not fulfilled, the real losers will be these people, who could suffer for years to come."[7] If Bill and Bill were to take the longer view, however, and acknowledge the connection between biotechnology and the run-amok cultural and economic conditions that have raised bioengi-neering to the level of a life-and-death imperative, they would understand that the development and use of this technology are but symptoms of a much older problem. The Pandora's box of genetic engineering is open and will remain open as long as we ignore the underlying forces that are pushing this technology forward. Make no mistake, Bill Gates is wrong: the real losers in the biotech revolution will turn out to be everyone. When whatever limited gains that can be made from genetic manipulation have been exhausted and the purity of nature has been spoiled in the most dangerous way, where will that leave us?

Much the same applies to the Human Genome Project. Here we see that the technology is far along in its development, which most everyone realizes, Bill Joy included. However, we also see a failure on the part of Joy and others to deconstruct the false imperatives that justify the exploitation of human nature. In the case of the human genome, the goal is essentially one of eugenics: to clean up the gene pool so as to make a better breed of humans, hopefully with the added bonus of doubling or tripling the human life span (just think what this will do to world population!). Naturally, nobody wants such things as cancer, diabetes, heart disease, depression, or schizophrenia, but few people recognize that there are much safer and more promising ways of dealing with these problems than through the manipulation of the genome, the most important of them being prevention. Once again, there is a general failure to acknowledge the larger forces that influence the prevalence of most of these problems. Again, this Pandora's box was opened as soon as we opted to take a technological attitude toward "solving" what are ultimately social and economic (rather than biological) problems. It is because we ignore or fail to recognize the underlying historical forces that drive our technological choices that we are losing control over technology, including the very technologies Joy fears could one day lead to grave ecological, biological, or human disasters.

Looking at the complexity, power, and portability of new information-based technologies, Joy also fears that humans could fall into a life-and-death struggle with machines. He is not a neo-Luddite, but on this subject he cites the most famous one of our time, Ted Kaczynski—the Unabomber:

What we do suggest is that the human race might easily permit itself to drift into a position of such dependence on the machines
that it would have no practical choice but to accept all of the machines' decisions. As society and the problems that face it become
more and more complex and machines become more and more
intelligent, people will let machines make more of their decisions
for them, simply because machine-made decisions will bring better results than man-made ones.[8]

It is interesting how many writers today begin by citing the words
of Ted Kaczynski.[9] As expressed in this passage, quoted from the
so-called Unabomber Manifesto, Joy fears a future in which humans no longer run the show. The ultimate outcome would seem to
be the one identified in *The Matrix,* where our unrestrained technological pursuit of artificial intelligence and virtual reality has somehow fused together, with us humans being taken prisoner by the
virtual machine. While I share a similar concern, I also believe that
Joy fails once again to link the possibility of such a future with the
realities of the present. The intelligent network of computing systems that could one day control the world already exists in a less obvious form today, as part of the *network society.*

The notion of a network society comes from Manuel Castells's
trilogy on the information age, the first volume of which is *The Rise
of the Network Society* (1996). Here he defines this society as

characterized by the globalization of strategically decisive economic activities. By the networking form of organization. By the
flexibility and instability of work, and the individualization of
labor. By a culture of real virtuality constructed by a pervasive,
interconnected, and diversified media system. And by the transformation of material foundations of life, space and time, through
the constitution of a space of flows and of timeless time, as expressions of dominant activities and controlling elites.[10]

Let's break this down into its parts.

Castells sees a world in which the economic imperatives are global ones. This means a narrowing down of economic independence and freedom throughout the world.

Castells also suggests that organizations in this global sphere are decentralized, flexible, and highly networked. A full-page ad in *The New York Times* describes the scenario: "For multinationals with complex global needs, to smaller companies with global aspirations. The communications revolution is underway, and, together, we will make sure your company is on the winning side."[11] This networking means an increase of world markets and their control by multinational corporations. It also means that we are moving toward such a heightened degree of centralization, thanks in no small part to computerization, computer networking, and the Internet, that one or a few individuals can exert a huge influence over financial institutions—both legally (e.g., through economic speculation) and illegally (through cyberterrorism). A 1995 article in *Business Week* states, "In this new market . . . billions can flow in or out of an economy in seconds. So powerful has this force of money become that some observers now see the hot-money set becoming a sort of shadow world government—one that is irretrievably eroding the concept of the sovereign powers of a nation state."[12]

Castells also sees the network society as a culture of real virtuality. As I have already mentioned, this means that you live in a world that is highly codified, even though you are not likely to have any awareness of the codification process that's under way.

Finally, Castells sees a transformation of the material foundations of life, space, and time under the control of highly rationalized systems supervised by powerful elites. As discussed in Part IV, this means that your life is torn from place, ritual, and permanence and resituated within a cybergeography defined by an infinite but placeless space.

In the "new economy" of the network society, we are essentially forced to inhabit a world in which the most significant decisions and changes in our lives are predetermined by self-replicating, global institutions whose logic, power, and life span far exceed those of even the most elite individuals who serve them.[13] Not only has the public interest been lost to the corporate interest, the corporate interest has become so automated in terms of computer networking, economic imperatives, and the protection of stockholder interests that it has taken on a life of its own. As David Korten writes in *When Corporations Rule the World:*

> The story of economic globalization is only partly a tale of the fantasy world of Stratos dwellers and the dreams of global empire builders. There is another story of impersonal forces at play, deeply embedded in our institutional system—a tale of money and how its evolution as an institution is transforming human societies in ways that no one intended [and] toward ends that are inimical to the human interest. It is a tale of the pernicious side of the market's invisible hand, of the tendency of an unrestrained market to reorient itself away from the efficient *production* of wealth to the *extraction* and *concentration* of wealth.[14]

Castells notes in his second volume, *The Power of Identity,* that a new society emerges when there is a transformation in the "relationships of production, in the relationships of power, and in the relationships of experience."[15] In the information age, production is reoriented toward information, a new order of power is seized through globalization, and the nature of experience is transformed through digitization. What is impressive about these three interlocking facets of the network society—and why they suggest that Bill Joy's feared future is now—is how well they cooperate in destroying the local fabric of material civilization, organized primarily in ethical terms, by replacing it with an immaterial pseudocivilization, organized primarily in economic ones.

With systems of mass media linked to systems of information linked to systems of finance linked to systems of education linked to systems of employment linked to systems of government policy, individuals are caged within a set of hyperrationalized imperatives. Those who are fortunate enough to earn a reasonable living will usually have enough material distractions and diversions to obscure the iron bars of the cage. We may even convince ourselves that the Internet and the information age will soon usher in a new renaissance, with power being redistributed to the masses. In truth, the trajectory of the network society is in just the opposite direction, so much so, in fact, that it's hard to imagine that a transfer of power to the level of computer intelligence would really make a difference. Is it not becoming less and less clear whether people—any people—are actually in control of the institutions of government, of corporations, of health care, of the media? And if so, wouldn't having so-called intelligent machines in control of the network society at least make it obvious? I believe so. I also believe it would lead to what is the only real solution to the domination of the future by high technology, which is one Bill Joy cannot even imagine. This is a political, technological, and industrial revolution in which the globally networked society is torn down and broken into pieces, followed by a rebuilding of decentralized communities that operate according to a principle of participatory democracy. In such a context, advanced technologies would not be obliterated; rather, they would be employed in a manner that would aid in the self-sufficiency of individual communities or regions.

Of course, such a revolutionary turn away from digitopia would not be imaginable if Joy's worst fears were realized, with the human race replaced by sentient robots. There is, however, an even more imminent and obvious danger. It's true that reconstruction of a valid democracy is not likely to be carried out by robots, but neither is it likely to be carried out by a nation of people who are themselves becoming a kind of sentient robot. Each day we are faced with an even more one-dimensional "economic man," all of whose wants are programmed by abstract hyperrealities and all of whose needs are satisfied by a global nervous system. Here, as Lewis Lapham has suggested, "The individual voice and singular point of view disappears into the chorus of a corporate and collective consciousness."[16] The thinking person who wants to stand in the way of "progress" is driven to the margins of existence. And it's here that we find individuals like the Unabomber, who, rather than conforming to the madness he saw in his own society, escaped into another kind of madness. Instead of inner destruction (of his beliefs), he seemed propelled toward outer destruction.

This brings us to another of Bill Joy's fears, also expressed in a passage quoted from Kaczynski, in which the Unabomber describes the possibility of a few elites controlling the machines that control everyone else:

Of course, life will be so purposeless that people will have to be biologically or psychologically engineered either to remove their need for the power process or make them "sublimate" their drive for power into some harmless hobby. These engineered human beings may be happy in such a society, but they will most certainly not be free. They will have been reduced to the status of domestic animals.[17]

This "brave new world" of an engineered happiness already exists today, and on quite a massive scale. As I noted in the essay "Pharmacological Aid," the Prozac revolution is a revolution not in science but in social philosophy, where the mission of pharmacology has been transformed from the traditional aim of restoring wellness to the postmodern aim of making us "better than well." In other words, an absolute standard of psychological well-being has been abandoned, replaced by a relative standard driven by the hyperrealities of a life unhinged by lifestyle capitalism. All this fits within a single cybernetic philosophy in which those who can afford to manipulate and manufacture mind and body may do so, while all others are turned away. Both sides will lose in this cybernetic turn, however, since human health and contentment are impossible to achieve in the cultural pursuit of human perfection. In fact, the entire system seems to be iatrogenic, with the cure becoming the ultimate sickness.

OUR FANTASTIC VOYAGE

wild ride or technological tailspin:

can we tell the difference?

W̲hen trying to imagine where the digital future will take us, I have the same experience that people have when they think about the outer limits of the Universe. That is, I find it hard to imagine that there can be any end to it, at least an end that stops short of digitopia. It is perhaps for this reason more than any other that I feel we are on a trajectory into a great unknown. Looking back at where technology has already taken the human race and how totally unimaginable this fantastic voyage would have seemed to people who lived millennia ago, it seems as though the past provides us with little intuition of what's to come. We as a society have a great capacity to develop digital and other related technologies, but this capacity seems inversely related to our capacity to envision the future these technologies will usher in. Other countries also show this pattern, but because they are not as strong in regard to the former (technology), they are not as blind in regard to the latter (vision)—or vice versa, as the case may be. In fact, when we look at the digital age through a wider lens, placing it within the larger context of all our technological pursuits in America, we see much the same imbalance.

American politicians and journalists call the United States the world's peacemaker, yet we are in fact the leading developer and exporter of military technology. We excel beyond any other nation in making arms, and we seem ignorant about how this implicates us in the world's conflicts and wars. We also excel beyond any other nation in making medical technology, yet we have nowhere near the most advanced system of health care. Spending more than any other nation on medicine (per capita), we seem ignorant about how to use this technology and spending to keep ourselves from getting sick in the first place. Much the same applies to education. Billions of dollars are being spent on computer and other "learning" technologies, but we have no conception of how these technologies will, or even could, help eradicate ignorance and illiteracy.[1] In the United States, we work more hours per year than people in any other Western country, we buy more guns than people in any other Western country, we imprison more of our own people than does any other country,[2] and we are the only Western country that executes its own citizens. Where, in other words, is all our wealth and technology taking us?

For all our ingenuity and innovation, we seem to find ourselves in a technological tailspin. But why? Why is there such a disconnection between our intelligence in the domain of technological affairs and our intelligence in the domain of human affairs? The answer seems to lie in our privileging of all that is economic and technological over all that is social and existential, in the hope that the former will somehow trickle down into the latter. But when the development, marketing, and uses of technology are driven primarily by profit margins, technology does not evolve to serve people's long-term needs.

Two examples: With the serendipitous discovery and success of the drug Viagra, the pharmaceutical industry is now investing billions of dollars per year researching and developing drugs that have only "lifestyle" purposes.[3] The title of an article in *The Nation* makes the point: "Millions for Viagra, Pennies for Diseases of the Poor: Research Money Goes to Profitable Lifestyle Drugs."[4] Allowed to put profits ahead of people, pharmaceutical companies are so cash-happy that they spend billions of dollars pushing their drugs. Sometimes this consists of one drug company competing against another; at other times it consists of the drug industry constructing the very problem that the drug is then said to serve (e.g., constructing shyness as a "disease" to sell the drug Paxil).[5] In 1998 and 1999, the pharmaceutical industry spent an estimated $10 billion on advertising alone; in 1997, it spent an estimated $74.8 million in lobbying the federal government—more than any other industry.[6] It is estimated today that the pharmaceutical industry spends an average of $12,000 per American physician pushing its wares.[7] Again, when the development, marketing, and use of technology are driven by the profit motive, technology does not evolve to serve people's needs.

A similar example is the realm of digital technology, where billions of dollars more are spent developing and promoting other "lifestyle" products. The profit motive in this industry is much like that of the pharmaceutical industry, always pandering to people's desire for a technological quick fix for every woe or whim. Devices such as mobile phones and wireless e-mail, for example, are said to liberate us from place by providing increased freedom and flexibility. There are freedom from the office, freedom to communicate instantly, freedom to perform multiple tasks simultaneously, freedom to be anywhere yet send and receive calls or messages. Users of these lifestyle solutions, like the users of the drug companies' lifestyle solutions, are slowly realizing, however, that with these so-called freedoms comes a certain enslavement. In the digital realm, for example, workplaces are now instituting policies of constant *digital reach,* mandating how often workers must check their voice mail and e-mail, and whether or when they can turn off their mobile phones and pagers.[8] A Sprint ad: "Want to make your business more productive? Make it more portable."[9] An IBM ad: "New bandwidth. New wireless. New standards. New demands. New expectations. New work."[10] A *New York Times* headline: "E-Mail You Can't Outrun."[11] A *Guardian* headline: "Living for the Company." A *Finan-*

cial Post headline: "Reflecting on Portable Technology's Effect: Liberating and Enslaving All at Once."[12]

Despite the growing surveillance and digital monitoring of people's lives, few seem to notice how the digital world is closing in. In the realm of communication media, first we had the telegraph, then the town phone, the party line, the home phone, the pager, the mobile phone, and now wireless e-mail. The computer realm looks much the same: first there was the mainframe, then the PC, the laptop, the Pocket PC, the PDA, now the wearable computer, and soon the implanted, neural-based microchip. If this is the digital future, it's clear that freedom is what's being bought and sold, although not exactly in the way you have been led to believe. In the name of freedom, you are losing the freedom to be engrossed in a single activity without distraction, you are losing the freedom to escape work when not at work, and you are losing the basic freedom to be left alone. The encroachment of the former set of freedoms over the latter should come as no surprise, however, as there's little profit margin in preserving the unplugged realm.

Both examples illustrate how technology becomes an end in itself, rather than a means that serves a coherent vision of basic human needs. If, in the process, "lifestyle" technologies also happen to indulge certain psychological wants, well, that's all for the economic better, since these wants then become dependencies, creating a perpetual market for even newer technologies. But is there not a certain contradiction in saying that the new and improved technologies will further simplify our increasingly complicated lives?

This may sound cynical, but what I'm driving at is not cynical at all. What if, in contrast to what I have just described, the ethos surrounding technology were reversed? Instead of the corporate world using the realm of mass media and popular culture to exploit and promote psychological needs, what if our basic social and psychological needs actually determined the development and uses of technology? We have become accustomed to being swept up by the next new thing, it's true, but this is not an indelible aspect of human nature. The real cynicism here is the hypercapitalist belief that a self-serving, competitive profit motive is better aligned with human nature and human needs than is a public-serving, cooperative people motive.

If the technology of tomorrow were redirected to the service of human ends above all others, we would live in a truly exciting time. We could imagine a better life of family, friends, community, nature, work—and then we could tap our phenomenal capacity for innovation to meet those ends. Who would decide these ends? Here we face the same problem. U.S. democracy, from the municipal to the federal level, is in such an impotent state that envisioning any such scenario sounds wildly idealistic. And once again, this is because the process of democracy has been co-opted by the profit motive. That the political process is driven by money is only part of the story, however. More important is that people are so overwhelmed in their fragmented, frenetic, plugged-in lives that they have no capacity to participate in civic life. The result is that government has been professionalized and sold off to corporate interests. Instead of suffering an ineffective state apparatus that attempts to dictate our every thought and move, we suffer a highly effective corporate (and mass media) apparatus that does essentially the same. Serving the nation-state is less sexy than engaging in the conquest of cool, but the outcome is much the same: power remains mostly in the hands of the few, thought remains mostly a product of the mass media, people remain caught in a mode of physical and/or psychological survival, and the human spirit remains little more than an undeveloped potential.

In terms of slowing down and reversing our ever-accelerating pursuit of digitopia, my conclusion is that overcoming technological temptation requires that we overcome our social and political poverty; overcoming this poverty requires that we rethink the nature of economy; and rethinking the nature of economy requires that we reconsider the nature of our own human nature.

In writing this book, I have attempted to do just this—to clarify the nature of our human nature, and to show how it gives rise to the look of the new digital you. I have tried to show that because of media technology the world has been falling into abstraction for a very long time. I have tried to show that we as human beings thrive best under conditions that support a balance between individual identity and social connectedness, even though we have failed to preserve this balance. I have tried to show that, in indulging our senses, we have been lured out of the social realm and into an artificial one. I have tried to show that we adapt to the drama, rhythm, and speed of electronic technologies, such that new technologies come to serve manufactured needs. I have tried to show that the world now being transformed by the digital information age is becoming all surface and no depth, and that quality, stability, and permanence have been replaced by quantity, motion, and change. And I have tried to show that if we as a society remain caught in the mythos of lifestyle capitalism that encourages only the roles of consumer, patient, and worker, we will continue down the path to a fully wired (and wireless) world.

The coming digital world will take us to a time that has, literally, no place. The name of this placeless place is *digitopia*.

Acknowledgments

I would like to acknowledge some of the intellectual influences on this project, namely the works of Marshall McLuhan, Jean Baudrillard, and Jacques Ellul. This book is at best a footnote to their insights into the dialectic between the psychological and the technological. I would also like to acknowledge my able editors at Random House, Janelle Duryea and Jon Karp, as well as some friends who provided important feedback during the writing of this book, including Paul Fleckenstein, Tony Dolan, Linda Wong, Edward Hardy, and Dallas Hansen. Finally, I would like to dedicate this book to Dan, Mike, and Cathy—my siblings and friends.

Notes

PART I. GOING DIGITAL

INTRODUCTION

1. Cited in W. Terrence Gordon, *Marshall McLuhan: Escape into Understanding* (New York: Basic Books, 1997).
2. As of September 2000, Media Matrix estimated that 7.4 million households in the United States had mobile phones, pagers, and/or personal digital assistants; see "Meet the New Web. Same as the Old Web," *The New York Times* (September 28, 2000): D1.
3. From "Everyday Life in the Modern World." Quoted in Stuart Ewen, *All Consuming Images: The Politics of Style in Contemporary Culture* (New York: Basic Books, 1988), p. 24.

DIGITALLY MASTERED

1. Electronic monitoring devices can also be implanted. See Katherine Mieszkowski, "Put That Chip Where the Sun Don't Shine," Salon.com (September 7, 2000).
2. On this theme, see Christian Parenti, *Lockdown America* (New York: Verso, 2000).
3. Stephen Jay Gould, "Only Human, We Are Neither Alone nor Divisible," *Forbes ASAP,* www.forbes.com (October 2000).
4. These statistics, many of which were quoted by Sony employees, vary; however, all agree that the Emotion Engine technology, unique to the PlayStation 2, is a dramatically faster machine than was PlayStation 1. See Yoshiko Hara and Will Wade, "Driven by 128-Bit Emotion Engine," *Electronic Engineering Times* (October 11, 1999): 4; Steven Levy, "Here Comes PlayStation 2," *Newsweek* (March 6, 2000): 54; Stephanie Strom, "Why PlayStation 2 Isn't Child's Play," *The New York*

Times (October 16, 2000): C1, C4; Doris Jones Yang, "Leaving Moore's Law in the Dust," *U.S. News and World Report* (July 10, 2000): 37–38.

5. This problem was related to a strobing effect that has since been eliminated from cartoons. But the general point still stands: new technologies are pushing the realm of simulated reality to its sensory limits, and it's not at all clear what the consequences will be, either today or in the future.

6. Paul Keegan, "Culture Quake," *Mother Jones* (November–December 1999): 42–49, pp. 42, 46.

7. Bill Joy, "Why the Future Doesn't Need Us," *Wired* (April 2000): 238–262.

FOUR DNA BASES, TWENTY-SIX LETTERS,
A ZERO, AND A ONE

1. Richard Dawkins, *River out of Eden: A Darwinian View of Life* (New York: Basic Books, 1995), p. 12.

2. Eric C. Lander, "In Wake of Genetic Revolution, Questions About Its Meaning," *The New York Times* (September 12, 2000): D5.

3. Note that alphabets such as ours, the Roman alphabet, differ in this way from ideographic systems of writing, including Chinese, since the latter are not reducible to individual signs that create words through different combinations.

4. Eric A. Havelock, *Origins of Western Literacy* (Toronto: Ontario Institute for Studies in Education, 1976).

5. Walter Ong, *Orality and Literacy* (New York: Methuen, 1982), p. 28.

6. Ibid., p. 87. At least at the present time, Mandarin is not necessarily taught everywhere in China, and it is not at all clear how long it will be before universal literacy exists in China in a single language, which may be Mandarin but could also be Cantonese.

7. In some technological systems, this is done as binary code, whereas in other systems, it may be in a numerical code; for example, computers rely exclusively on the former while digital communications rely on the latter.

8. This is really only the first step in a long process that may be slow in producing meaningful results. The reason is that the role of genes in human development and disease is much more complex than is generally appreciated.

THE ONE AND ONLY REALITY

1. The concepts of a digital matrix, cyberspace, and jacking in all have their origins, I believe, in William Gibson's classic science fiction novel *Neuromancer* (New York: Ace Books, 1984). Some of these ideas are also apparent in Marge Piercy's *Woman on the Edge of Time* (New York: Knopf, 1976) and *He, She, and It* (New York: Knopf, 1991).

2. James J. Gibson, "Adaptation, After-effect and Contrast in the Perception of Curved Lines," *Journal of Experimental Psychology*, 16 (1933): 1–31; James J. Gibson, *The Senses Considered as Perceptual Systems* (Boston: Houghton Mifflin, 1966); James J. Gibson, *The Ecological Approach to Visual Perceptions* (Boston: Houghton Mifflin, 1979); see also James J. Gibson and Eleanor J. Gibson, "Perceptual Learning: Differentiation or Enrichment?," *Psychological Review*, 62 (1955): 32–41.

3. Daniel J. Boorstin, *The Image: A Guide to Pseudo-events in America* (New York: Harper Colophon, 1961), pp. 37, 240.

4. Interview with Phil Tippett in Iain Boal, *Resisting the Virtual Life: The Culture and Politics of Information* (San Francisco: City Lights Books, 1995), p. 256.

5. Thomas F. Cash et al., "The Nature and Extent of Body-Image Disturbances in Anorexia Nervosa and Bulimia Nervosa," *International Journal of Eating Disorders*, 22 (1997): 107–126; Donald A. Williamson and Barbara A. Cubic, "Equivalence of Body Image Disturbances in Anorexia and Bulimia Nervosa," *Journal of Abnormal Psychology*, 102 (1993): 177–181; see also Ophira Edut, ed., *Adiós, Barbie: Young Women Write About Body Image and Identity* (Seattle: Seal Press, 1998).

THE REAL AND THE TRUE

1. Albert Borgmann, *Crossing the Postmodern Divide* (Chicago: University of Chicago Press, 1992), p. 3.

2. *Forbes ASAP*, www.forbes.com (October 2, 2000).

3. See S. Moscovici, "The Generalized Self and Mass Society," in *Societal Psychology*, ed. H. T. Himmelweit and G. Gaskell (London: Sage, 1990), pp. 66–91.

SURVIVING *SURVIVOR*

1. Lewis Mumford, *The Pentagon of Power* (New York: Harcourt Brace Jovanovich, 1964), p. 414.

2. This neologism comes from Jean Baudrillard, *Simulacra and Simulation* (Ann Arbor: University of Michigan Press, 1994), p. 16.
3. Jean Baudrillard, *The Perfect Crime* (London: Verso, 1996), p. 27.
4. Sherry Turkle, "Constructions and Reconstructions of the Self in Virtual Reality," in *Electronic Culture*, ed. Timothy Druckrey (New York: Aperture, 1996), pp. 354–365.

DIGITAL MECHANICS

1. Dave Grossman, *On Killing* (New York: Back Bay Books, 1996).
2. Ibid., p. xix.
3. This quote comes from David Barstow and Sarah Kershaw, "Teenagers Accused of Killing for a Free Meal," *The New York Times* (September 7, 2000): A1, A29; see also David Barstow et al., "A Killing, and the Anguish of Families of the Accused," *The New York Times* (September 9, 2000): A1.
4. The American Psychiatric Association report, first issued in 1992, was entitled "Big World, Small Screen"; the AMA's report, "Physician's Guide to Medical Violence," was issued in 1996; and the NIMH report, "Television and Behavior: 10 Years of Scientific Progress and Implications for the Eighties," was first issued in 1982.
5. David E. Rosenbaum, "Violence in Media Is Aimed at Young, F.T.C. Study Says," *The New York Times* (September 11, 2000): A1.
6. Ibid.
7. Sharon Waxman, "Click. Bang. It's Only a Game," *The Washington Post* (May 27, 1999): C1.

PART II. THE LONG JOURNEY INTO DIGITOPIA
A SHORT HISTORY OF THE DIGITAL SELF

1. Marshall McLuhan, *Understanding Media: The Extensions of Man* (Cambridge, Mass.: MIT Press, 1996), p. 308.
2. Oliver Wendell Holmes, "The Stereoscope and the Stereograph," *Atlantic Monthly* (June 1859): 738–748, p. 748.
3. See Walter Ong, *Orality and Literacy* (New York: Methuen, 1982), chapter 4.
4. Cited in Paul Keegan, "Culture Quake," *Mother Jones* (November–December 1999): 42–49.
5. I do not mean to suggest that there are not other ways of organizing this

history. The influence of radio and broadcasting could be emphasized more, as could be the distinction between film and television, only the latter of which uses analog technology.

6. Daniel J. Boorstin, *The Image: A Guide to Pseudo-events in America* (New York: Harper Colophon, 1961), p. 3. Boorstin also gives the well-known quote from Max Frisch: "Technology . . . the knack of so ar-ranging the world that we don't have to experience it."

7. Jay Chiat, "Illusions Are Forever," *Forbes ASAP,* 130 (October 2, 2000): 139.

8. From an interview on *Charlie Rose* (September 21, 2000), PBS.

9. Howard Rheingold, *Virtual Reality* (New York: Summit Books, 1991), p. 192.

UNPLUGGED MEDIA

1. Note as well that each of these phases of selfhood brought with it its own discipline of study, which for these six selves include archaeology, anthropology, linguistics, history, media studies, and the computer/in-formation sciences, respectively.

2. Claude Lévi-Strauss, *The Savage Mind* (Chicago: University of Chi-cago Press, 1961).

3. From a poem by O. Mandelstam, cited in Lev Semenovich Vygotsky, *Thought and Language* (Cambridge, Mass.: MIT Press, 1962), p. 119.

4. Jack Zipes, *When Dreams Come True: Classical Fairy Tales and Their Tradition* (New York: Routledge, 1999), p. 1.

5. David Abram, *The Spell of the Sensuous* (New York: Pantheon, 1996), p. 156.

6. Vygotsky, *Thought and Language.*

7. Walter Ong, *Orality and Literacy* (New York: Methuen, 1982), p. 78.

8. Philip Marchand, *Marshall McLuhan: The Medium and the Messenger* (Cambridge, Mass.: MIT Press, 1989), p. 131.

9. Ibid.

10. The statistics on printing are from Hugh Thomas, *An Unfinished His-tory of the World* (London: Pan, 1980).

11. From *Playboy* (March 1969), as quoted in Marchand, *Marshall McLuhan.*

12. Ong, *Orality and Literacy,* pp. 14–15.

PLUGGED-IN MEDIA

1. On this, see Douglas S. Robertson, *The New Renaissance: Computers and the Next Level of Civilization* (New York: Oxford University Press, 1998).
2. Jacques Ellul, *The Technological Society* (New York: Vintage, 1954/1964 trans.), p. 325.
3. Richard DeGrandpre, *Ritalin Nation: Rapid-Fire Culture and the Transformation of Human Consciousness* (New York: Norton, 1999).
4. In fact, early films could get by on motion alone, although once this effect wore off, people wanted narrative as well.
5. Stuart Ewen, *All Consuming Images: The Politics of Style in Contemporary Culture* (New York: Basic Books, 1988), p. 25.
6. Susan Buck-Morris, *Dreamworld and Catastrophe: The Passing of Mass Utopia in East and West* (Cambridge, Mass.: MIT Press, 2000), p. 104.
7. VR technology was originally developed by VPL Research, created by Jaron Lanier, who coined the term "virtual reality" in the 1980s; VPL was sold to Sun Microsystems in 1992.
8. See Robert D. Putnam, *Bowling Alone* (New York: Simon & Schuster, 2000), chapter 13.
9. Daniel J. Boorstin, *The Image: A Guide to Pseudo-events in America* (New York: Harper Colophon, 1961), p. 19.

THE COMING OF DIGITAL AGE

1. Austin Bunn, "The Rise of the Teen Guru," *Content* (July–August 2000): 66–69, p. 66.
2. Matt Richtel, "Choosing a Salary or Tuition: Some Young Computer Experts Say No to College," *The New York Times* (September 7, 2000): D1.
3. Roger Fillion, "Fast Forward," *Context* (August–September 2000): 53–58, pp. 53, 55.
4. Research by Richard Nisbett et al., to be published in *Psychological Review*, as summarized in Erica Goode, "How Culture Molds Habits of Thought," *The New York Times* (August 8, 2000): F1, F4.
5. See, e.g., Y. Hong et al., "Multicultural Minds: A Dynamic Constructivist Approach to Culture and Cognition," *American Psychologist,* 55 (July 2000): 709–720.
6. For an ethnographic study of this, see the PBS documentary "Lost Children of Rockdale County" (1999).

PART III. THE PSYCHOLOGY OF THE DIGITAL AGE

A DIGITAL ETHOS

1. Jean Baudrillard, *The Perfect Crime* (London: Verso, 1996), p. 17.
2. Leary later went on to advocate virtual reality as a liberating force, making some dubious assumptions. See Timothy Leary, "The Cyberpunk: The Individual as Reality Pilot," in *Storming the Reality Studio,* ed. Larry McCaffery (Durham, N.C.: Duke University Press, 1992), pp. 245–258.
3. Robert Nozick, *Anarchy, State, and Utopia* (New York: Basic Books, 1974), p. 42.
4. Robert Nozick, "The Pursuit of Happiness," *Forbes ASAP,* www.forbes.com (October 2000).
5. Ibid.
6. Of course, if they were aware of the digital matrix, it would no longer produce an identical neurophysiological experience; this is because the knowledge would change the experience.

THE SAD AND LONELY WORLD OF CYBERSPACE

1. W. Terrence Gordon, *Marshall McLuhan: Escape into Understanding* (New York: Basic Books, 1997), p. 196.
2. Philip Marchand, *Marshall McLuhan: The Medium and the Messenger* (Cambridge, Mass.: MIT Press, 1989), p. 140.
3. Frederick E. Allen, "When Sex Drives Technological Innovation," *American Heritage* (September 2000): 20.
4. Jacques Ellul, *The Technological Society* (New York: Vintage, 1954/1964 trans.), p. 146.
5. On the questionable role of the Internet in supporting American democracy, see David Corn, "Filegate.gov," *Wired* (October 2000).
6. These observations on the Internet derive largely from "What the Internet Cannot Do," *The Economist* (August 19, 2000).
7. Amy Harmon, "Sad, Lonely World Discovered in Cyberspace," *The New York Times* (August 30, 1998): A1.
8. Robert Kraut et al., "Internet Paradox: A Social Technology That Reduces Social Involvement and Psychological Well-being?," *American Psychologist,* 53 (October 2000): 1017–1032.
9. This study, conducted in 1999 by the Stanford Institute for the Quantitative Study of Society, was cited in Kalle Lasn and Bruce Grierson, "Malignant Sadness," *Adbusters* (June–July 2000): 28–39.
10. For example, see R. E. Anderson et al., "Relationship of Physical Ac-

tivity and Television Watching with Body Weight and Level of Fatness Among Children," *Journal of the American Medical Association,* 279 (1998): 938–943.

11. This is based on comparisons between people's self-reports of satisfaction with being online versus longitudinal measures of psychosocial functioning; compare, e.g., J. E. Katz and P. Aspden, "A Nation of Strangers?," *Communications of the ACM,* 40 (1997): 81–87; and Robert Kraut et al., "Internet Paradox."

VIRTUAL REALITY SHAPES THE MIND IN ITS OWN IMAGE

1. David Abram, *The Spell of the Sensuous* (New York: Pantheon, 1996).
2. Originally published in *The Sciences,* this essay appears in Robert M. Sapolsky, *The Trouble with Testosterone* (New York: Touchstone, 1997), p. 38.

A DIGITAL VIRUS

1. In some cases, parenting has become such a low priority and such a disaster for some parents that they have turned their kids over to foster care. See Somini Sengupta, "Many Frustrated Parents Turn to Foster Care as Their Only Option," *The New York Times* (September 1, 2000): A21.
2. Kalle Lasn and Bruce Grierson, "Malignant Sadness," *Adbusters* (June–July 2000): 32.
3. On this, see William Leach, *Land of Desire: Merchants, Power, and the Rise of a New American Culture* (New York: Pantheon, 1993); quote from James Rorty, cited in Richard Pells, *Radical Visions and American Dreams* (New York: Harper & Row, 1973).
4. Robert D. Putnam, *Bowling Alone* (New York: Simon & Schuster, 2000).
5. Mark S. Granovetter, "The Strength of Weak Ties," *American Journal of Sociology,* 78 (1973): 1360–1380; see also Lisa F. Berkman and Thomas Glass, "Social Integration, Social Networks, Social Support, and Health," in *Social Epidemiology,* ed. Lisa F. Berkman and Ichiro Kawachi (New York: Oxford University Press, 1993), pp. 137–174.
6. Putnam cites Berkman and Glass, ibid.
7. Putnam makes no reference to psychopathology or drugs such as Prozac or Ritalin in his text despite their clear linkage with the breakdown of the social sphere.

8. Cross-National Collaborative Group, "The Changing Rates of Major Depression: Cross Cultural Comparisons," *Journal of the American Medical Association,* 268 (1992): 3098–3105. See also the work of social epidemiologist Myrna Weissman and colleagues: Myrna M. Weissman et al., "Cross-National Epidemiology of Major Depression and Bipolar Disorder," *Journal of the American Medical Association,* 276 (1999): 293–299; Myrna M. Weissman et al., "The Cross-National Epidemiology of Panic Disorder," *Archives of General Psychiatry,* 54 (1999): 305–309; Myrna M. Weissman et al., "Cross-National Epidemiology of Obsessive Compulsive Disorder," *Journal of Clinical Psychiatry,* 55 (suppl.) (1994): 5–10.

9. Putnam, *Bowling Alone,* p. 100.

10. J. E. Katz and P. Aspden, "A Nation of Strangers?," *Communications of the ACM,* 40 (1997).

11. Sally McGrane, "Long-Distance Romance, Web-Enabled," *The New York Times* (August 31, 2000): D11.

12. Ali H. Mokdad et al., "Diabetes Trends in the U.S.: 1990–1998," *Diabetes Care,* 23 (2000): 1278–1283.

13. See A. Mokdad et al., "The Spread of the Obesity Epidemic in the United States, 1991 to 1998," *Journal of the American Medical Association,* 282 (1999): 1519–1522.

14. D. Biersdorfer, *The New York Times* (September 28, 2000): D1.

15. As reported by Jeffrey Kluger in "The Diabetes Explosion," *Time* (September 4, 2000): 23.

16. Putnam, *Bowling Alone,* p. 245.

FIGHT AND FLIGHT

1. From Franklin's CBC Massey Lectures, published as *The Real World of Technology* (Toronto: CBC Enterprises, 1990), p. 11.

2. On how the profession of psychology serves the economic status quo, see Isaac Prilleltensky, "Psychology and the Status Quo," *American Psychologist,* 44 (1989): 795–802; and Isaac Prilleltensky, *The Morals and Politics of Psychology: Psychological Discourse and the Status Quo* (Albany: State University of New York Press, 1994).

3. Philip Cushman, "Why the Self Is Empty: Toward a Historically Situated Psychology," *American Psychologist,* 45 (1990): 599–611.

4. Hakim Bey, "The Information War," in *Virtual Futures,* ed. Joan Broadhurst Dixon and Eric J. Cassidy (New York: Routledge, 1998), p. 5.

5. Oliver James, *Britain on the Couch: Why We're Unhappier Compared with 1950 Despite Being Richer* (London: Century, 1997).
6. This neologism comes from Oliver James.
7. For this concept, I am indebted to Dallas Hansen.
8. Robert Wright, "The Evolution of Despair," *Time* (August 28, 1995); Robert Wright is also the author of *The Moral Animal* (New York: Pantheon, 1994).
9. Richard DeGrandpre, *Ritalin Nation: Rapid-fire Culture and the Transformation of Human Consciousness* (New York: Norton, 1999).

THE DRAMA OF THE DIGITAL SELF

1. Jessica Benjamin, *The Bonds of Love* (New York: Pantheon Books, 1988), p. 12.
2. Robert Kegan, *The Evolving Self: Problem and Process in Human Development* (Cambridge, Mass.: Harvard University Press, 1992); Alice Miller, *The Drama of the Gifted Child* (New York: Basic Books, 1981); see also D. W. Winnicott, *Mother and Child: A Primer of First Relationships* (New York: Basic Books, 1957).
3. R. D. Laing, *The Divided Self: An Existential Study in Sanity and Madness* (Baltimore: Penguin, 1967), p. 65.

DIGITAL DREAMS, CONCRETE REALITIES

1. Arthur Kleinman and Alex Cohen, "Psychiatry's Global Challenge," *Scientific American* (March 1997): 86–90; see also Richard Levins, "Is Capitalism a Disease?: A Report on the Crisis in U.S. Public Health," *Monthly Review* (September 2000): 8–33.
2. William A. Vega et al., "Lifetime Prevalence of DSM-III-R Psychiatric Disorders Among Urban and Rural Mexican Americans in California," *Archives of General Psychiatry,* 55 (1999): 771–778.
3. William Leach, *Land of Desire* (New York: Pantheon, 1993), p. 5.
4. Neil Postman, *Technopoly: The Surrender of Culture to Technology* (New York: Vintage, 1993), p. xii.
5. A look at the ten bestselling drugs shows that the majority of them are for problems the high prevalence of which is either psychologically or behaviorally driven, including problems of obesity, heart disease, diabetes, and asthma.

6. From a figure caption in *Adbusters* (Summer 1999).
7. Richard Wainwright, "Our Empty Desires," *Adbusters* (June–July 2000): 25.
8. Maggie Jones, "Cure It with Drugs," *The New York Times Magazine* (October 15, 2000): 88–89:
9. "It seems that every time an old memory is pulled into consciousness, the brain takes it apart, updates it and then makes new proteins in the process of putting the memory back into long-term storage," writes Sandra Blakeslee in *The New York Times;* "Brain-Updating Machine May Explain False Memories," *The New York Times* (September 5, 2000): F7.
10. See, e.g., Daniel B. Wright and Elizabeth F. Loftus, "How Misinformation Alters Memories," *Journal of Experimental Child Psychiatry,* 71 (1998): 155–165; Elizabeth F. Loftus, "Creating False Memories," *Scientific American* (September 1997): 70–76.
11. *Forbes ASAP* (October 2, 2000): 139.
12. Daniel J. Boorstin, *The Image: A Guide to Pseudo-events in America* (New York: Harper Colophon, 1961), p. 3.
13. This comparison of nomad and citizen comes from Lewis Lapham; see, e.g., his introduction to Marshall McLuhan, *Understanding Media: The Extensions of Man* (Cambridge, Mass.: MIT Press, 1964/1996).

FEELING OH, SO ANALOG IN AN ALL-TOO-DIGITAL AGE

1. As one critic points out, "Those who have turned away from traditional value systems find themselves left with no immediate obvious replacement. And so, industry and advertising have rushed in to fill the gap with a corporate-sponsored morality that places brand loyalty above all others. The introduction of advertising into school systems is a prime example: children are molded into loyal consumers of the future by targeted product placement, sponsorship, and education in the values of consumption." Adam Lammiman, "Whose Reality Is It Anyway?," *Adbusters* (June–July 2000): 18.
2. Richard DeGrandpre, *Ritalin Nation: Rapid-Fire Culture and the Transformation of Human Consciousness* (New York: Norton, 1999); see also Richard J. DeGrandpre, "ADHD: Serious Psychiatric Problem or All-American Cop-out? A Debate Between Richard J. DeGrandpre and Stephen P. Hinshaw," *Cerebrum* (Summer 2000): 12–38.

3. Steven Levy, "Here Comes PlayStation 2," *Newsweek* (March 6, 2000): 54.
4. Paul Keegan, "Culture Quake," *Mother Jone,* (November–December 1999): 44.
5. Interview with Phil Tippett in Iain Boal, *Resisting the Virtual Life: The Culture and Politics of Information* (San Francisco: City Lights Books, 1995), p. 256.
6. See, e.g., Lynette Lamb, "Where Do the Children Play?," *Utne Reader* (September–October 1994): 24–25.
7. See, e.g., Alex Kuczynski, "Advertising: Radio Squeezes Empty Air Space for Profit," *The New York Times* (January 6, 2000): A1.

THE INCREDIBLE SHRINKING ATTENTION SPAN

1. "Big Issue III," *Forbes ASAP,* www.forbes.com (November 30, 1998).
2. On how, for example, "architecture has accommodated itself to a distracted way of life," see Herbert Muschamp, "Peeking Inside Other People's Dream Houses," *The New York Times* (September 19, 1999): 37.
3. For example, a survey by the Pew Charitable Trust showed that 74 percent of Americans over fifty who do not have Internet access have no interest in it; see "A Study of the Wired World Finds Dropouts and No-shows," *The New York Times* (September 28, 2000): D3.
4. The quote in this *New York Times* ad is attributed to *Internet Week.*

PHARMACOLOGICAL AID

1. Peter Kramer, *Listening to Prozac* (New York: Viking, 1997).
2. David J. Rothman, "Shiny Happy People," *The New Republic* (February 14, 1994): 34–38.
3. Maggie Jones, "Cure It with Drugs," *The New York Times Magazine* (October 15, 2000).
4. Richard J. DeGrandpre, "Surgeon General's Report Is Laudable but Misleading," *Mental Health Weekly* (January 10, 2000): 4; Richard J. DeGrandpre, "Just Cause?," *The Sciences* (March–April 1999): 14–18.
5. "Beyond Prozac," *Newsweek* (February 7, 1994).
6. David Healy, *The Antidepressant Era* (Cambridge, Mass.: Harvard University Press, 1997).
7. Sharon Begley, "One Pill Makes You Larger, One Pill Makes You Small," *Newsweek* (February 7, 1994): 36–40.

8. Michael D. Lemonick, "The Mood Molecule," *Time* (September 29, 1997): 74.
9. See Erica Goode, "Once Again, Prozac Takes Center Stage," *The New York Times* (July 18, 2000): F1; Joseph Glenmullen, *Prozac Backlash* (New York: Simon & Schuster, 2000).
10. A magazine essay entitled "Melancholy Nation" notes, "All but lost in the clamor are some dispiriting facts: Prozac has not turned out to be a magic bullet against depression, and the problem is now worse than ever. In fact, many who study depression say that we are entering an 'Age of Melancholy,' where people are getting depressed at younger and younger ages, with episodes that are severe and frequent. By some measures, depression has already doubled since World War II, an increase not simply due to greater awareness, says Columbia University epidemiologist Myrna Weissman, but due also to factors such as more stress, fewer family and community ties, even nutritional deficiencies." Joannie Schrof and Stacey Schultz, *U.S. News and World Report* (March 8, 1999): 56–63.
11. Quoted in Neil Postman, *Technopoly: The Surrender of Culture to Technology* (New York: Vintage, 1993).
12. Julian Stallabrass, "Empowering Technology: The Exploration of Cyberspace," *New Left Review,* 211 (May–June 1995): 7.

PART IV. THE GEOGRAPHY OF DIGITOPIA
LIVING IN TIMELESS TIME AND PLACELESS SPACE

1. Martin Heidegger, *Being and Time* (New York: Harper, 1962, trans.).
2. For example, in Jerome Bruner, *Acts of Meaning* (Cambridge, Mass.: Harvard University Press, 1990), Bruner writes of a "renewed cognitive revolution—a more interpretive approach to cognition concerned with 'meaning-making,' one that has been proliferating these last several years in anthropology, linguistics, philosophy, literary theory, psychology, and, it would almost seem, wherever one looks these days" (p. 2).
3. "The Lure of Silence," *The Economist* (August 19, 2000): 27.
4. Danny Hillis, *Forbes ASAP,* www.forbes.com (October 2, 2000).
5. It also means that old-fashioned place is getting uglier than ever. On this see Lisa Guernsey, "The Future Is Here, and It's Ugly: A Spreading Techno-blight of Wires, Cables and Towers Sparks a Revolt," *The New York Times* (September 7, 2000): D1, D7.

6. Julian Stallabrass, "Empowering Technology: The Exploration of Cyberspace," *New Left Review* (May–June 1995): 15.
7. Manuel Castells, *The Rise of the Network Society* (Oxford, Eng.: Blackwell, 1996); David Harvey, *The Condition of Postmodernity: An Enquiry into the Origins of Cultural Change* (Oxford, Eng.: Blackwell, 1989).
8. Rosabeth Moss Kanter, "Simultaneity," *Forbes ASAP,* www.forbes.com (November 30, 1998).
9. Marshall McLuhan seemed to anticipate this, writing in *Understanding Media,* "If the work of the city is the remaking or translating of man into a more suitable form than his nomadic ancestors achieved, then might not our current translation of our entire lives into the spiritual form of information seem to make of the entire globe, and of the human family, a single consciousness?" Marshall McLuhan, *Understanding Media: The Extensions of Man* (Cambridge, Mass.: MIT Press, 1964/1996).

CONSTRUCTING DIGITOPIA

1. Michael Pollan, "Feeding Frenzy," *The New York Times Magazine* (December 12, 1999): 43–44.
2. On this, see Robert A. Freitaas, Jr., "Say 'Ah!,' " *The Sciences* (July–August 2000): 26–31, pp. 27, 31; Ed Regis, *Nano* (Boston: Little, Brown, 1995).
3. Ray Kurzweil, "Will My PC Be Smarter Than I Am?," *Time* (June 19, 2000): 82–85.
4. Michael D. Lemonick, "Will Tiny Robots Build Diamonds One at a Time?," *Time* (June 19, 2000): 94–97.
5. Freitaas, "Say 'Ah!,' " pp. 27, 31.
6. Igor Aleksander, "A Neurocomputational View of Consciousness," in *From Brain to Consciousness: Essays on the New Sciences of Mind,* ed. Steven Rose (Princeton, N.J.: Princeton University Press, 1998), p. 182; see also John W. Donahoe and David C. Palmer, *Learning and Complex Behavior* (Needham Heights, Mass.: Allyn and Bacon, 1994); John W. Donahoe et al., "Selectionist Approach to Reinforcement," *Journal of the Experimental Analysis of Behavior,* 58 (1993): 17–40; Gerald M. Edelman, *Neural Darwinism: The Theory of Neuronal Group Selection* (New York: Basic Books, 1987); Gerald M. Edelman, *Bright Air, Bril-*

liant Fire: On the Matter of the Mind (New York: Basic Books, 1992); D. E. Rumelhart et al., eds., *Parallel Distributed Processing,* vol. 1 (Cambridge, Mass.: MIT Press, 1986).

7. Betty Hart and Todd R. Risley, *Meaningful Differences in the Everyday Experience of Young American Children* (Baltimore: Paul H. Brooks, 1995).

8. On this, see D. Barnes, "Stimulus Equivalence and Relational Frame Theory," *The Psychological Record,* 44 (1994): 91–124; Richard J. De-Grandpre et al., "Emergent Equivalence Relations Between Interoceptive (Drug) and Exteroceptive (Visual) Stimuli," *Journal of the Experimental Analysis of Behavior,* 58 (1992): 9–18; J. M. Devany et al., "Equivalence Class Formation in Language-Able and Language-Disabled Children," *Journal of the Experimental Analysis of Behavior,* 46 (1986): 243–257; Murray Sidman, *Equivalence Relations and Behavior* (Boston: Authors Cooperative, 1994).

9. See, e.g., Ernst Mayr, *Toward a New Philosophy of Biology: Observations of an Evolutionist* (Cambridge, Mass.: Harvard University Press, 1988); Elliot Sober, *The Nature of Selection* (Chicago: University of Chicago Press, 1984).

10. See G. J. Whitehurst and M. C. Valdez-Menchaca, "What Is the Role of Reinforcement in Early Language Development?," *Child Development,* 59 (1988): 430–440.

11. Donahoe and Palmer, *Learning and Complex Behavior;* David C. Palmer and John W. Donahoe, "Essentialism and Selectionism in Cognitive Science and Behavior Analysis," *American Psychologist,* 47 (1992): 1344–1358.

12. Susan Greenfield, "How Might the Brain Generate Consciousness?" in *From Brain to Consciousness,* pp. 210–227, p. 214; Susan Greenfield is also the author of *The Private Life of the Brain* (New York: John Wiley and Sons, 2000).

13. Palmer and Donahoe, "Essentialism and Selectionism"; Richard J. De-Grandpre, "A Science of Meaning," *American Psychologist* (July 2000): 721–739.

14. Spelled out, these are: computerized axial topography, electroencephalography, magnetic resonance imaging, and positron emission topography.

15. Richard J. DeGrandpre, "Just Cause?," *The Sciences* (March–April, 1999): 14–18.

16. John Horgan, *The Undiscovered Mind* (New York: Free Press, 1999).

17. Marvin Minsky, *The Society of Mind* (New York: Simon & Schuster, 1986).
18. George Johnson, "The Ultimate, Apocalyptic Laptop," *The New York Times* (September 5, 2000): D1.
19. Stephen J. Ceci, *On Intelligence . . . More or Less* (Englewood Cliffs, N.J.: Prentice Hall, 1990).
20. Ray Kurzweil, "Will My PC Be Smarter Than I Am?"
21. Many other variations on this theme are imaginable, although I have attempted to stay within the realm of existing modes of technology. As for the original mind that is left behind, who knows? This is as much a technological question as a philosophical one, given the possibility of multiple minds for the same person. Perhaps the original mind would be lost in the mapping of the clone. Perhaps the original would be diseased, and so it would simply be left behind to fade (e.g., with Alzheimer's). Perhaps because of an ecological or technological disaster, masses of individuals would be euthanized after having their minds downloaded. Or perhaps the mind would commit the ultimate heresy and sell its new self into slavery. Again, who knows?

PART v. THE FUTURE OF THE FUTURE
THE (BILL) JOYS OF TECHNOLOGY

1. Bill Joy, "Why the Future Doesn't Need Us," *Wired* (April 2000): 237–262.
2. Ibid., p. 243.
3. Kevin Kelly, *Out of Control: The New Biology of Machines, Social Systems, and the Economic World* (Reading, Mass.: Addison-Wesley, 1994), p. 4.
4. For a clear example, see Joe Thornton, *Pandora's Poison: Chlorine, Health, and a New Environmental Strategy* (Cambridge, Mass.: MIT Press, 2000).
5. Joy, "Why the Future Doesn't Need Us," p. 256.
6. Ibid., p. 244.
7. Bill Gates, "Will Frankenfoods Feed the World?," *Time* (June 19, 2000).
8. From the so-called Unabomber Manifesto; quoted in Joy, "Why the Future Doesn't Need Us," p. 239.
9. For other prominent examples, see Robert Wright, "The Evolution of Despair," *Time* (August 28, 1995); Ray Kurzweil, *The Age of Spiritual Machines* (New York: Viking, 2000).

10. Manuel Castells, *The Rise of the Network Society* (Oxford, Eng.: Blackwell, 1996), p. 1. He continues, "This new form of social organization, in its pervasive globality, is diffusing throughout the world, as industrial capitalism and its twin enemy, industrial statism, did in the twentieth century, shaking institutions, transforming cultures, creating wealth and inducing poverty, spurring greed, innovation, and hope, while simultaneously imposing hardship and instilling despair. It is indeed, brave or not, a new world."

11. Concern Communications Company, *The New York Times* (October 5, 2000): A9.

12. Quoted in David C. Korten, *When Corporations Rule the World* (West Hartford, Conn.: Kumarian Press, 1995); from "Hot Money," *Business Week* (March 20, 1995).

13. In this context, it is absurd to think that we will be any more effective in controlling machine intelligence, should it emerge in a significant way. This is just what is proposed by the Carnegie Mellon University robotics scientist Hans Moravec, who sees robots as a superior life-form to humans and welcomes their taking over all industrial labor in the world. As *The New York Times* noted, "The last significant act of humans, [Moravec] said, would be the passing of laws to ensure that robot-run companies acted in the interest of humans." In truth, we cannot even get human-run corporations to act in the long-term interests of humans. Quote from Kenneth Chang, "Can Robots Rule the World? Not Yet," *The New York Times* (September 12, 2000): D4.

14. Korten, *When Corporations Rule the World,* p. 188.

15. Manuel Castells, *The Power of Identity* (Oxford, Eng.: Blackwell, 1997), p. 340.

16. Lewis H. Lapham, introduction to Marshall McLuhan, *Understanding Media: The Extensions of Man* (Cambridge, Mass.: MIT Press, 1964/1996), p. xxi.

17. Joy, "Why the Future Doesn't Need Us," p. 239.

OUR FANTASTIC VOYAGE

1. A *New York Times* article states, "But while at least 96 percent of public schools now have Internet access, according to the National Center for Education Statistics, it is often unclear how that access is being used to enhance learning. . . . And some educators and parents question how much computers and the Internet really help children learn." Bonnie

Rothman Morris, "A Day in the Life of the Wired School" (October 5, 2000): D1, D8; see also Jane M. Healy, *Failure to Connect: How Computers Affect Our Children's Minds* (New York: Simon & Schuster, 1999).

2. Early in the year 2000, the United States jailed its two millionth inmate. The United States makes up 5 percent of the world's population but contains 25 percent of the world's prison inmates. See Duncan Campbell, "US Jails Two Millionth Inmate," *The Guardian Weekly* (February 17, 2000): 1, 32.

3. Julia Finch, "Lifestyle Drugs Gain Allure," *The Guardian* (August 20, 1999): 31.

4. Ken Silverstein, "Millions for Viagra, Pennies for Diseases of the Poor: Research Money Goes to Profitable Lifestyle Drugs," *The Nation* (July 19, 1999): 13–18.

5. See, e.g., M. Cottle, "Selling Shyness: How Doctors and Drug Companies Created a 'Social Phobia' Epidemic," *The New Republic* (August 2, 1999): 24–29; A. Raghunathan, "A Bold Rush to Selling Drugs to the Shy," *The New York Times* (May 18, 1999): C1, C2; see also Richard J. DeGrandpre, "Just Cause?," *The Sciences* (March–April, 1999): 14–18.

6. See Jeff Gerth and Sheryl Gay Stolberg, "Drug Industry Nurses Ties to Wide Range of Groups," *The New York Times* (October 5, 2000): A1, A23; David D. Kirkpatrick, "Selling Happiness," *New York* (May 15, 2000).

7. Kirkpatrick, ibid.

8. For a spoof on PDAs and digital reach, see Christopher Buckley, "Wireless Shrugged," *Time* (May 29, 2000).

9. *The New York Times* (October 5, 2000): A32.

10. *The New York Times* (October 3, 2000): C15.

11. *The New York Times* (September 21, 2000): D1.

12. Grace Casselman, "Friend or Foe? Two-Faced Mobility; Reflecting on Portable Technology's Effect: Liberating and Enslaving All at Once," *Financial Post* (February 21, 2000): E1.

About the Author

RICHARD DEGRANDPRE is a psychologist and independent science writer and has been published in a great variety of both professional and popular publications, including *American Psychologist, The Sciences, Common Knowledge, Psychology Today, Cerebrum,* and *Adbusters.* His first book, *Ritalin Nation: Rapid-Fire Culture and the Transformation of Human Consciousness,* is now available in paperback.

About AtRandom.com Books

AtRandom.com books are original publications that make their first public appearance in the world as e-books, followed by a trade paperback edition. AtRandom.com books are timely and topical. They exploit new technologies, such as hyperlinks, multimedia enhancements, and sophisticated search functions. Most of all, they are consumer-powered, providing readers with choices about their reading experience.

AtRandom.com books are aimed at highly defined communities of motivated readers who want immediate access to substantive and artful writing on the various subjects that fascinate them.

Our list features literary journalism; fiction; investigative reporting; cultural criticism; short biographies of entertainers, athletes, moguls, and thinkers; examinations of technology and society; and practical advice. Whether written in a spirit of play or rigorous critique, these books possess a vitality and daring that new ways of publishing can aptly serve.

For information about AtRandom.com Books and to sign up for our e-newsletters, visit www.atrandom.com.